Percy Maylam's

The Kent
Hooden Horse

Percy Maylam's
The Kent
Hooden Horse

RICHARD MAYLAM, MICK LYNN & GEOFF DOEL

The
History
Press

DEDICATION

The editors would like to dedicate this book to their long-suffering (in the cause of folklore) wives: Sophie Maylam, Kathy Lynn and Fran Doel.

Front cover photograph: The Deal Hoodeners, 1909. (H. B. Collis)

Back cover photograph by Sophie Maylam, from left to right: Alan Hibbert (Tonbridge Hoodener: Waggoner), Mick Lynn (Tonbridge Hoodener and co-editor of book), Richard Maylam (great-nephew of Percy Maylam and co-editor of book), Lord Kingsdown KG, (H.M. Lord Lieutenant of Kent), Mrs Tricia Shephard MBE (chairman of the Association of Men of Kent & Kentish Men), Geoff Doel (as Tonbridge Hooden Horse, co-editor of the book), and, in front, Fran Doel (Tonbridge Hoodener: Mollie).

First published 2009
Reprinted 2023

The History Press
97 St George's Place, Cheltenham,
Gloucestershire, GL50 3QB
www.thehistorypress.co.uk

British Library Cataloguing in Publication Data.
A catalogue record for this book is available from the British Library.

ISBN 978 0 7524 4997 5

Typesetting and origination by The History Press
Printed and bound in Great Britain by TJ Books Limited, Padstow, Cornwall.

Trees for Life

CONTENTS

Acknowledgements	6
Foreword	7
Editor's Note	9
Note to the New Edition	10
The Kentish Hooden Horse and its Analogues	11
The Hooden Horse: An East Kent Christmas Custom by Percy Maylam	19
Introduction	20
Chapter I	22
Chapter II	27
Chapter III	48
Chapter IV	57
Chapter V	81
Chapter VI	93
The Hooden Horse Footnotes	107
The Revival of the Custom	110
Short Bibliography for the two Hooden Horse articles	113
The Custom of Gavelkind in Kent by Percy Maylam	114
Bibliography for Gavelkind	124
Index	126

ACKNOWLEDGEMENTS

The editors would like to thank the following people and organisations:

Mrs Elizabeth Hamilton for Maylam family photos and information.

Mrs Sophie Maylam and Mr John C. Maylam for photo.

The Association of Men of Kent & Kentish Men & the Kent Archaeological Society for supporting talks by the editors at meetings in various pats of Kent and for booking The Tonbridge Mummers & Hoofteners at Christmas socials and the Kent County Show.

The Education Officer of the Maidstone Museum, Hayley McMechan for booking the editors to launch the book with an illustrated talk.

The Tonbridge Mummers & Hoofteners (past & present members) for thirty years of enjoyable performances.

The staff at Tonbridge & Folkestone Libraries and Maidstone & Deal Museums

And to the following individuals who have provided information and helpful discussions over the years: Alan Austen, Tony Deane, Fran Doel, Mark Lawson, Simon Evans and the late Jack Hamilton.

FOREWORD

Great Uncle Percy would be pleased and amazed to think that the work he undertook to publish the *Hooden Horse* in 1909 would still interest enough people for it to be republished nearly 100 years later. The reason for the book in the first place was that Percy Maylam was concerned that the tradition should no be lost for all time. He said 'the custom is fast decaying and I was therefore anxious to leave a record on a permanent medium'. That permanent medium, in the shape of his book, achieved its objective as it has encouraged people like Mick Lynn and Geoff and Fran Doel to continue to practice the Hoodening tradition while at the same time they are collecting folk music and mummers' plays.

Great Uncle Percy was born into a long line of Kentish farmers at Pivington Farm, Pluckley, in 1865. He was admitted as a solicitor of the Supreme Court in 1890 and he married Kate Pearch, who was born in Hastings. They had two sons, Robert and James. Percy lived a busy life as a solicitor in Canterbury. He was a coin collector and he enjoyed his cricket, but he is best known as an amateur historian, becoming a member of the Kent Archaeological Society in 1892. He subsequently died in Canterbury in 1939. He had traced his family's history and privately published *Maylam Family Records* in 1932, and in it Percy relates how his father William told how his father, Clark, was born at Parker Farm between Warehorne and Ham Street. Clark Maylam had in turn related that people were very concerned about their personal safety during the times when Napoleon was expected to invade this country, probably through Romney Marsh. Clark Maylam's parents and his brothers and sisters at Parker Farm never went to bed without seeing that the waggon and horses were ready to take them and their valuables in land, in case the French invaded.

One of Percy Maylam's other practical involvements in local history was in connection with the ancient Kentish custom of Gavelkind. He knew of the 1836 bill to abolish Gavelkind, but the bill was withdrawn before it became enacted due to the level of local objection. He in turn objected to the proposed abolition of the custom when it was set out in the Real Property Bill of 1913 and in that year he produced a twelve-page pamphlet arguing the case to leave traditions as they had been for the last 900 years – an early case of 'if it ain't broke don't fix it'! The retention of this old tradition was won by the men of Kent and Kentish men when they surrounded William the Conqueror near Greenhithe, some time after the Battle of Hastings. It was there that they negotiated that the people of Kent would recognise him as their king if he would let the custom of Gavelkind continue.

It is from this agreement that the Kent motto of *Invicta* came about, i.e. 'unconquered'. And so in Kent, William I is not referred to as William the Conqueror, but as William of Normandy or William the Bastard.

And so now in this era of great change, I am pleased that Dr Doel and Dr Lynn are giving us the opportunity to read the 1913 publication on Gavelkind as an appendix to the republication of the Hooden Horse.

The *Hooden Horse* was published in 1909, but with only 303 copies, and so serious researchers have found the books difficult and expensive to come by. It seems fitting that the centenary of the publication of the book should be celebrated by it being published again to increase its availability.

The original edition of the *Hooden Horse* went to many quarters of the world and I wish this edition a similar success as it reawakens a tradition in Kent which is perhaps still only just under the surface.

Richard Maylam

EDITOR'S NOTE

In attempting to revise the text of a publication that is highly revered in certain circles, I have striven to use an extremely light touch to ensure that as much of the original as possible shines through. After all, it was Percy Maylam that saw these events and did the research, not me.

However, there were a few errors in the original book and the use of some punctuation of that time, especially that of quotation marks, has changed enough to make it seem odd and distracting at times to the modern reader.

Thus I hope you can rest assured that you are as near to the original texts written by Percy Maylam as modern methods allow.

Dr Mick Lynn

NOTE TO THE NEW EDITION

The publishers suggested changing Percy Maylam's original title slightly to emphasise Percy and Kent (for booksellers to classify), rather than the more geographically limiting East Kent.

THE KENTISH HOODEN HORSE & ITS ANALOGUES

Introductory article by Dr Geoff Doel

According to Parish and Shaw's *A Dictionary of the Kentish Dialect* (1888):

> In the custom of Hoodening, a farmer used to annually send round the neighbourhood the best horse in the charge of the waggoner. Later, instead, a man was used to represent the horse, being supplied with a tail and with a wooden (pronounced 'ooden' or 'hooden') figure of a horse's head and plenty of horsehair for a mane. The horse's head was fitted with hob-nails for teeth; the mouth being made to open by means of a string and in closing made a loud crack.

It is unlikely that the Reverend Parish, Vicar of Selmeston in Sussex (he is also the author of a book on Sussex dialect), or his colleague had ever seen a Hooden Horse, although some of the features such as hobnails and the method of opening and closing the mouth are perceptive details. The accuracy of Parish and Shaw's research is also testified by their correct emphasis on the use of a carved wooden head in Kent, as opposed to a skull as used in several other midwinter British horse disguise customs. These details show they have gone to sources other than Reverend Samuel Pegge's *An Alphabet of Kenticisms (1735-1736)*, a source giving the earliest reference to the Hooden Horse, as well as furnishing them with considerable other Kentish material; Pegge was vicar of Godmersham. As we should expect from experts in dialect, the correct pronunciation is carefully and helpfully specified by Parish and Shaw. But other details are lacking in their description. There is no reference to the covering or sacking (often a hop sack), or to the time of year, or to the demographic local of east Kent, or to the other characters associated with the custom. And the mention of the custom succeeding the use of a real horse is puzzling and lacks corroboration. Significantly, the past tense is used. To folklorists of 1888, the custom was perceived of as a dead or dying relic of the past, as near death as the horse in the series of *Poor Old Horse* songs found all over the country, themselves possibly widespread survivors of a well-established tradition of midwinter horse disguise customs in the British Isles:

> When I was young and in my prime
> And in my stable lay,
> They gave to me the very best corn
> And eke the choicest hay.
> Poor old horse! Poor old mare!

My master used to ride me out
O'er many a gate and style,
O'er many a hedge and ditch I've gone,
And borne him many a mile.
Poor old horse! Poor old mare!

My feeding once was of the best,
The sweetest of sweet hay,
That ever grew in a green field
When fields with flowers were gay.
Poor old horse! Poor old mare!

Now I am old and quite done for
And fit for naught at all,
I'm forced to eat the sour grass
Upon the churchyard wall.
Poor old horse! Poor old mare!

Then lay my tott'ring legs so low
That have run very far,
In following the hounds and horn
O'er turnpike gate and bar.
Poor old horse! Poor old mare!

My hide I'll to the huntsman give,
My shoes I'll throw away;
The dogs shall eat my rotten flesh
And that's how I'll decay.
Poor old horse! Poor old mare!
(Baring Gould & Cecil Sharp: *English Folk-Songs for Schools*)

Percy Maylam had the good fortune to witness the custom as a young man in the 1880s, so for him it was a living Kent custom, though one, like Gavelkind, which was under threat. His approach to the subject was both admirable research through nineteenth-century books, periodicals and local papers, plus field research that led him to witness and interview three extant traditions of the Hooden Horse – at St Nicholas at Wade, Walmer and Deal. His enthusiasm, detailed descriptions and clear photographs both encouraged the continuation of the custom at the locations he visited (for example, by encouraging the adding back in of the recently departed 'Mollie' to the St Nicholas at Wade tradition) and enabled the custom to be accurately revived in the twentieth century. His classic study is also impressive for its separation of fact from speculation as to the origins and significance of the custom.

The Edwardian period was a fertile time for collecting English folk customs. Cecil Sharp was adding a detailed examination of the Morris dance tradition in several volumes to his phenomenal folk song collections. Member of Parliament Sir Benjamin Stone was involved in building an extensive photographic collection of folk customs and Reginald Tiddy was soon to begin his research into the Mummers plays. The Folk Lore Society, with whom

Maylam was associated, was actively encouraging research into customs, and its president reviewed his book most positively in the *Folk Lore Journal* for 1910. Sir James Frazer was encouraging comparative folklore studies and speculations of their possible religious origins in his seminal *The Golden Bough* (12 vols 1890-1905). All this was just in the nick of time, as the rural workforce was losing interest in and contact with their own extensive cultural heritage. The professional classes (Percy was a solicitor) began to take an interest and to record these customs for posterity, both encouraging their continuance for a while and providing photographs and records to enable later revivals during the Second Folk Revival of the 1960s and 1970s, when a new generation sought to re-forge links with its rural heritage.

Percy Maylam was interested in the distinctive Kentishness of the Hooden Horse (as with the survival of Gavelkind), but as a cultured and widely read man (as were all these early folklorists), he was also aware of the wider connotations, such as the likely links with the midwinter British, and indeed European, horse cults, and he draws attention to these in his book. In Britain we find remnants of midwinter horse disguise customs in the Llair Bane of Ireland and Tommy the Pony in Dorset (both with wooden heads) and with skull-horses in Cornwall, South Wales (the Mari Lwyd), Lancashire, Cheshire and the borders of Yorkshire, Derbyshire and Nottinghamshire. With the exception of Cheshire (where some thirty village Mummers plays featured a skull-horse over the Hallowe'en period – one at Antrobus still surviving), the rituals are near Christmas. Indeed the Mari Lwyd is said to be the mare turned out of the stable to make way for Mary and Joseph, which sounds like a medieval legend invented to explain away a custom that did not quite fit into the Christian ethos. Percy Maylam was also aware of the extensive traditions of vibrant stallions and hobby horses in May traditions, and his papers contain two early postcards of the Minehead hobby horse tradition. All these ritual seasonal customs have been admirably described, compared and analysed in Dr E.C. Cawte's *Ritual Animal Disguise* (Brewer, 1978).

The Frazerian and Edwardian interest in possible religious (pagan or Christian) and early superstitious and sympathetic magic elements in many seasonal customs was initially enthusiastically followed by the Folk Lore Society and in publications by Violet Alford and Margaret Murray. This form of investigation was undoubtedly both obsessive and excessive, and has been rejected by most more-recent folklorists. It is possible that in their understandable reaction against Margaret Murray, modern folklorists have thrown out the baby with the bathwater, because the kind of balanced approach to the subject of religious/ritualistic origins offered by Maylam, and his well-read contemporaries, is surely worth at least considering in the case of the Hooden Horse. The word 'pagan' is a problem in this context as many modern folklorists react hysterically to it and demonise with emotional arguments those who suggest pagan elements in our folklore. The word in its Latin context actually means 'rural superstition', and it seems to me in this context paganism need not mean pre-Christian or denote some anti-Christian activity, but merely to invoke a set of ideas concerning the rural life force and ethos with seasonal and magical attributes which differ from, but often complement, the official religious views of the practitioners of the customs.

The attitude of many folklorists today would be to date the origin of the Hooden Horse from the first written record (1734) and give it a purely social context of evolution. This is a very simple approach and obviates the need for wider cultural or historical knowledge. But there is much circumstantial information and evidence in the case of the Hooden Horse (and many other seasonal customs) to suggest that it substantially pre-dates 1734, at least in antecedents, the evolution of the custom being rather more complex. There is of course a general absence of interest in, or reference to, folk customs before the growth of antiquarian interest in the eighteenth century.

The attachment of customs to significant calendar and seasonal dates, Midwinter/ Christmas in the case of the Hooden Horse, does suggest the possibility of a religious association. The Midwinter solstice was a crisis in nature with the sun's vigour at its lowest, darkness prevailing and the growth of vegetation ceasing. Midwinter rituals such as Apple Wassailing and the death and resurrection part of the Mummers play do strongly suggest the practice of sympathetic magic to re-energise the life force. It is possible that some such concept or ritual underlies the development of the Hooden Horse custom. Religious and ritualistic customs, as opposed to social customs, tended until recently to have male only performers, any female characters, such as the 'Mollie' in the Hooden Horse and the Judy in the Mari Lwyd, being taken by men. Cross-dressing is itself a known inducement to fertility in primitive cultures, though its survival is humorous in British folklore and folk drama. Even in a dramatic context, the male only preserve of the Hooteners suggests a certain antiquity, female dramatic parts being taken by men in England on the stage until 1660.

The Midwinter association of the Hooden Horse custom could of course relate to Christmas, either as associated with the Christian religion, or because this was a festive time where strange antics were more likely to be expected and rewarded. Another factor, suggested by Percy Maylam, is that the farm horses in Kent tended to be rested over Christmas, which gave the carters and others working with the horses on the farms free time to indulge in the custom and to earn some extra cash. This context would also provide an alternative scenario for the absence of female performers.

If the origins of the custom are religious on the other hand, apart from the death and resurrection element (quite muted in this custom), what is the significance of the horse? Archaeological evidence suggests that horse skulls have had ritual significance as far back as Stone Age and Bronze Age cultures, judging, for example, the use and alignment in burials; there is a Kentish example of this from Keston. The horse cult was particularly strong amongst the Celtic peoples as evinced by the carving of the Uffington White Horse (now securely dated as the late Bronze Age or Celtic period) and the story of Rhiannon in *Pwyll, Prince of Dyfed* in *The Mabinogion*. The Romano-Gallic peoples worshipped a horse goddess, Epona, and a number of statues and altars from her cult survive in Britain and Europe. Also, Tacitus in the first century AD records that the Germans kept white horses that were thought to be 'privy to the gods' counsels' and which were, therefore, used for the purpose of divination. The Vikings are recorded as using horses' skulls on poles to work magic. The souling plays at Antrobus and other Cheshire villages, which feature a horse's skull on a pole held by a man covered in sacking, could derive from Celtic or Scandinavian culture as there was extensive Norse settlement there. The horses heads used in these plays were regarded as good luck talismans and were often buried in the villages between the yearly performances. To steal the horse's head from another village would be to double the good fortune of one's own village during the coming year. Such a concept is unlikely to have been invented within the last two hundred years.

The Hooden Horse tradition in Kent relates particularly to the Isle of Thanet and to Walmer and Deal. Thanet was the earliest Anglo-Saxon settlement in Kent and, according to legends described in early Kentish & national chronicles, was given by the British King Vortigen to his Saxon *federati* led by Hengist and Horsa, whose names mean 'stallion' and 'mare' and could be indicative of a tribal Germanic horse cult. Horse disguise rituals survive in Germanic folk customs. To anyone living in Kent, such as Percy Maylam, and indeed myself, it is tempting to try to make some link between all this and the Hooden Horse, especially as the horse is an early symbol for the county of Kent, but none of this can of course be proven or disproved.

The widespread provenance of horse disguise customs and associated songs in England, and indeed in Europe, is another factor which suggests a certain antiquity in the customs, or at least a link between it and some earlier form.

Where all folklorists can agree, is in admiration for Percy Maylam's detailed descriptions of the three surviving variations of the Kent Hooden Horse custom in the Edwardian period, his helpful sociological and biographical analysis of the participants, and his questioning of them as to their knowledge of earlier stages of the tradition.

As we have seen, the Kentish Hooden Horse is distinguished from the Souling Horse of Cheshire and the Mari Lwyd ('The Pale Mare') of South Wales, by its carved wooden head. Several nineteenth-century sources talk of a dead horse's head being used, but these references all seem to derive from a single reference in the *European Magazine* of 1807, which Percy Maylam draws attention to. As with the other horse-disguise customs, a man covered in cloth or sacking takes the part of the horse, stooping to make a back, clasping a pole attached to the head and opening and closing the horse's jaws by means of a string. A 'waggoner' was in charge of the horse and the 'jockey' attempted to ride him. There were attendant musicians and, in common with the Mari Lwyd custom, a man disguised as a woman with a blackened face and besom broom (the 'Mollie'), often attended the horse as well. The 'sweeper' figure is frequently found at solstitial celebrations. In Shakespeare's *A Midsummer Night's Dream*, Puck sweeps with his broom at the end of the play, while the marriages are being consummated at the solstice, as part of a ritual to bless the progeny of the unions and to ensure they are born free from deformity:

...not a mouse
Shall disturb this hallowed house.
I am sent with broom before
To sweep the dust behind the door.
(Act V (i) 373-5).

Oberon explains the intention of the fairy procession immediately following Puck's actions:

To the best bride-bed will we,
Which by us shall blessed be;
And the issue there create
Ever shall be fortunate.
So shall all the couples three
Ever true in loving be;
And the blots of Nature's hand
Shall not in their issue stand:
Never mole, hare-lip, nor scar,
Nor mark prodigious, such as are
Despised in nativity,

Shall upon their children be.
(Act V (i) 389- 400)

This is an explained dramatic example of a sweep figure involved in sympathetic magic. In Yorkshire, groups of guisers used to sweep through houses unannounced with besom brooms at New Year and the sweeper is a common figure in the Mummers play.

The name 'Hooden' may relate to the hooded appearance of the horse. Percy Maylam discusses possible connections with the Anglo-Saxon god Woden and even Robin Hood! The pronunciation of the 'oo' sound in the Thanet dialect was close to the Germanic 'ü' and the 'h' was dropped, giving a pronunciation *üden*. As Dr Cawte points out in his seminal work *Ritual Animal Disguise*, were it named after the Germanic god Woden, one would expect the 'w' sound to have been retained in the east Kent dialect as in the Kent place name Woodnesborough, near Ash (thought to be named after Woden), or the day of the week 'Wednesday', which was certainly was named after the god.

There are a number of religious denunciations of animal disguise customs from early medieval Europe through to Puritan England, although the most famous reference in the Penitential of Archbishop Theodore has now been shown to be a late interpolation (see E.C. Cawte's *Ritual Animal Disguise* & Ronald Hutton's *Stations of the Sun*)

Maylam first saw the Hooden Horse while spending Christmases with his uncle at Gore Street, Monkton, from 1888 to 1892, and he vividly describes this in his book (see pp. 22-23). In 1905, Percy arranged to photograph a team of Hoodeners from Hale Farm, St Nicholas at Wade (between Margate and Canterbury). The men in the team were employed with the horses on the farm and Maylam explains that this was traditionally the case since it was the custom to bleed Kent farm horses just before Christmas and then let them rest before ploughing, which began after Plough Monday. Thus the men in charge of the horses had little to do work-wise for the period over Christmas and took out a mock horse instead. The photographic session was arranged out of season at Bolingbroke Farm, Sarre and the 'Mollie' (whose role had recently lapsed) was specially revived (the Hoodeners that Maylam saw at Gore Street, 1888 to 1892, has a 'Mollie'). No besom broom was immediately to hand and Maylam's first photograph shows 'Mollie' playing the triangle, while somebody was busy at work behind the scenes making the besom shown in his second photo.

Maylam interviewed men who had personal knowledge of the custom at St Nicholas extending back at least to the 1840s. His interest in the St Nicholas Horse came as a stimulus when, in common with the other Hoodening traditions, it was on the wane. A photograph survives of the team c. 1919 with a revival of 'Mollie' as a permanent fixture. Although the custom lapsed for a time, the village never forgot it and it was revived in 1966. Researcher Simon Evans has tape-recorded the reminiscences of the 'rider' in the photo, Tom West, who lived at St Nicholas all his life.

Three years later, Maylam visited the Christmas Eve festivities at the Walmer Hooders. Robert Laming and his brother, William, and son, Joseph, played the music and Harry Axon carried the horse. Maylam did not photograph the Walmer Hooders until the following March.

In 1909, Percy Maylam documented the Deal Hooders, whom he found to be only two in number at the time. The account he gives documents the considerable changes to the make-up and venues of one Hooden Horse Party over twenty years, and is a warning to anyone assuming a static custom in the past, though one would expect greater changes to the custom at the end of the nineteenth century than at the beginning of the century.

A charming account sent to me in the early 1980s by Mrs Naomi Wiffen of Edenbridge, who saw the Deal horse as a small girl and whose story adds much fascinating detail:

> I remember as a child being taken out on Christmas Eve to the High Street in Deal where the shops would be open very late, and it was the only time Deal children were allowed out in the evening, as parents were very strict. As we would be looking at the lighted shops, and listening to the people selling their wares, a horrible growl, and a long horse's face would appear, resting on our shoulder and when one looked round, there would be a long row of teeth snapping at us with its wooden jaws. It was frightening for a child. Usually, there would be a man leading the horse, with a rope, and another covered over with sacks or blankets as the horse.

The Deal Museum displays two accounts of the Hooden Horse at the turn of the century, one calling it the 'Green Horse' and mentioning that it was accompanied by hand-bell ringing. The other account is from an old lady who was a member of a Deal boatman's family and who calls it the 'Ogling Horse':

> Then there was the Ogling Horse, - the hooded horse of Queen Elizabeth's reign, a man under a sack, with a wooden head something like a horse with two large clappers for a mouth, the man clapped them together with a terrible noise but that was part of Christmas.

A letter to the *European Magazine* in 1807 (much re-used by later nineteenth-century folklorists) provides a reference to a dead horse's head being used and also mentions hand-bells and carols which, according to Maylam, were not a regular feature of the custom, though they are mentioned later in one of the Deal accounts quoted above:

> Also at Ramsgate, in Kent, I found they begin the festivities of Christmas by a curious procession: a party of young people procure the head of a dead horse, which is affixed to a pole about ten feet in length: a string is affixed to the lower jaw: a horse-cloth is also attached to the whole under which one of the party gets, and by frequently pulling the string, keeps up a loud snapping noise, and is accompanied by the rest of the party, grotesquely habited, with hand-bells: they thus process from house to house, ringing their bells, and singing carols and songs; they are commonly gratified with beer and cake, or perhaps with money. This is called, provincially, a Hodening, and the figure above described a Hoden, or Woden horse.

Other references mention the custom at Broadstairs, St Peter's, St Lawrence, St Nicholas, Acol, Monkton and Birchington, calling at the door and the 'old woman' sweeping the feet of those who answered the door. Perhaps the most interesting of the accounts collected by Maylam is that sent to the Church Times in 1891 concerning the custom in the 1840s (see p. 38).

Percy Maylam's ground-breaking investigation of the Hooden Horse custom has provided an inspiration, a focus and a context for the collection of old Hooden Horses and information on the custom. In my second essay at the end of this book, I will show how Percy Maylam's book has inspired substantial revivals of the custom.

The Bibliography for this article appears on p. 110.

THE HOODEN HORSE

AN EAST KENT CHRISTMAS CUSTOM.

By Percy Maylam, Canterbury

I can nou3te perfitly my pater-noster • as þe prest it syngeth,
But I can rymes of Robyn hood and • Randolf erle of Chestre.

Piers the Plowman
Passus v.401-2

Only 303 copies privately printed

INTRODUCTION

The chief object of an introduction is to afford an opportunity for apologies and explanations.

In the first place I must apologise for the delay in sending out this book. It was inevitable – after the issue of the prospectus I received a large number of letters containing additional information and suggestions requiring further research, with the result that in the end, it became necessary to rewrite a large portion of the book, and in particular, the whole of Chapters III and IV.

My next apology has reference to the prominent feature – the title – for it cannot fail to be noticed that 'the Hoodening Horse' of the prospectus has been altered to 'the Hooden Horse'. It was pointed out to me that the latter is primary form and the one in everyday use among the country folk, while the former merely appears in a few written description; with this I quite agree, hence the correction.

In any work which has been written at odd moments during a period of several years, inconsistencies, if not contradictions, are inevitable; these I have endeavoured to rectify; but nevertheless I find that on page 28 I criticise the term 'procession' which is used in the *European Magazine* to denote the 'going round' of the hoodeners, as being merited neither by the number of the party nor their movements, and yet throughout Chapter VI, in the translations from the German writers, I have myself used this word as the equivalent for the German 'Zug' or 'Aufzug'. For frailties such as this, one can only ask forbearance.

The extracts from Grimm's *Teutonic Mythology* on pages 83 and 92 of the text are taken from the translation by Stallybrass (1882); and the extracts for Strutt's *Sports & Pastimes of the People of England* are taken from the edition edited by J. C. Cox and published by Methuen (1903). For the translations from the German in Chapter VI I am myself responsible.

The illustrations are of course merely reproductions for ordinary photographic blocks, the photographs having been taken by Mr. H. B. Collis of Canterbury, but I wish to call attention to the paper upon which they have been taken off. The ordinary so-called art paper generally used is most objectionable for the purposes in which durability is of importance. When this paper is used, the picture is taken off, not on the paper itself (the fabric of which possesses little or no durability), but on the glazed gelatinous coating – a total absence of permanency is the inevitable result. It is indeed distressing to observe the quality of paper which nearly every archaeological and folklore society use, for the purpose of recording valuable illustrations (presumably for the benefit of posterity) of objects of antiquity, often brought to light only at great expense, or representations of fast decaying folk-customs; all these are reproduced on a medium which, so far from being available for posterity, will, in many cases, barely survive the present generation of writers. If it is thought that my charges are exaggerated, one has only to consult any independent paper maker or analytical chemist.

So far as I know there are no representations of the custom, the subject of this book, other that those photographs which are reproduced here; the custom is fast decaying, and I was therefore anxious to leave a record on a permanent medium, even if this meant some loss of detail. The paper used for the illustrations in this work represents the result of experiments made by Mr. H. Cremer, the manager of Messrs. Howard & Son's Paper Mill at Chartham, Kent, with a view to the production of a strong rag paper, capable of taking process block illustrations on the paper itself without the intervention of any gelatinous coating. My best thanks are due to Mr. Cremer, and also to the printer, Messrs. Cross and Jackman, for much care and a great deal of patience.

Most of those to whom I am indebted for assistance in obtaining information receive my acknowledgments in the text, but I feel bound here to express my gratitude to my uncle, Mr. F. de B. Collard of Minster Abbey, Thanet (under whose hospitable roof at Gore Street, Monkton, I first became acquainted with the hooden horse), for the many inquiries he has made for me; and to my old friend and former tutor, Professor Dr. Habersang of Bückeburg, from whom I first learned to take an interest in things Teutonic, or, as he would prefer them to be called – Germanic.

Before concluding, I feel the necessity for some general apology for having written so much on such a small subject, it is however better, thoroughly to hoe the small potato patch at one's door, rather than undertake the cultivation of a large farm without the necessary knowledge of agriculture. I fear notwithstanding, that my readers on coming to the end of the book, will wonder with the immortal Weller, whether it was worth going through so much to learn so little.

CANTERBURY
December, 1909.

CHAPTER I

INTRODUCTORY – SPELLING AND PRONUNCIATION – DESCRIPTION – HOODENING IN THANET – WALMER

A few stray references to the 'hooden' or 'hoodening' horse are to be found in print it is true, some in well known books on general English Folklore and some in works dealing only with Kent; the files of the local newspapers from time to time contain more or less accurate descriptions accompanied by guesses as to the meaning and origin of the custom. A very large number of the references to the custom in books are merely paraphrases of the description which is the best known owing to the fact that it has found its way into Hone's *Every Day Book*. Certainly no one account gives any indication of the wide spread area in Kent over which this custom was practised in comparatively recent times, a writer who is acquainted with the custom in Thanet appears ignorant of its existence outside the Island and vice versa. In these days Kent possesses so few genuine popular customs of this kind that we cannot afford to be indifferent to those still in existence. This is my excuse for my attempt to record the custom as now existing before it is utterly lost to us.

In bye-gone days I think it is probable that the hooden horse was to be found at Christmas in every village and hamlet, in fact in every large farm in that part of Kent, which I shall indicate more closely in a subsequent chapter. Even at the present day the custom is not restricted to Thanet.

I will first clear the ground by dealing with the spelling and pronunciation of the word. As regards spelling, the most general form of the word in print is 'hoden' ,but I have adopted the spelling 'hooden', as this form best represents the pronunciation, the vowel being long. The word 'hooden' rhymes with 'wooden' and not with 'sodden' as some writers appear to think.

In Thanet and those parts of Kent where the Thanet pronunciation prevails the first vowel 'oo' (upon which the stress lies) is the obscure diphthong 'ew' characteristic of Thanet. In print, the sound of this diphthong can best be explained by saying that, if not identical with, it closely resembles the German 'u' with the Umlaut – 'ü'. Therefore the pronunciation in Thanet of 'hooden' is 'üden' and 'hoodening' 'üdnen', the 'h' being dropped of course.

In the next place I will give a present day description of the custom as now hoodening (1) in Thanet and (2) at Walmer.

Hoodening in Thanet.   Anyone who has spent a Christmas in a farm-house in Thanet – it has been my good fortune to spend five – will not forget Christmas Eve; when seated round the fire, one hears the banging of gates and trampling of feet on the gravel paths outside (or, if the weather be seasonable, the more cheerful crunching of crisp snow), and the sound of loud clapping. Everyone springs up. saying, 'The hoodeners have come, let us go and see the fun'. The front door is flung open, and there they all are outside, the 'Waggoner' cracking his whip and leading the Horse (the man who plays this part is called the 'Hoodener'), which assumes a most restive manner, champing his teeth, and rearing and plunging, and doing his best to unseat the 'Rider', who tries to mount him, while the 'Waggoner' shouts 'whoa!' and snatches at the bridle. 'Mollie' is there also! She is a lad dressed up in woman's clothes and vigorously sweeps the ground behind the horse with a birch broom. There are generally two or three other performers besides, who play the concertina, tambourine or instruments of that kind. This performance goes on for some time, and such of the spectators as wish to do so, try to mount and ride the horse, but with poor success. All sorts of antics take place, Mollie has been known to stand on her head, exhibiting nothing more alarming in the way of lingerie than a pair of hobnail boots with the appropriate setting of corduroy trousers. Beer and largess are dispensed and the performers go further. Singing of songs or carols is not usually part of the performance and no set words are spoken [1]. In Thanet, occasionally, but not always, the performers, or some of them, blacken their faces. Years ago, smock frocks were the regulation dress of the party.

In a house which possesses a large hall, the performers are often invited inside; at times the horse uses little ceremony, and opening the door, walks in uninvited. In the bright light indoors, the performance, though the cause of much amusement, is deprived of all illusions, the crude make-up of the horse is glaringly apparent and we recognise the performers plainly, as the Bill or Tom of every day life, who look after the horses. Without doubt the Hoodeners are seen at their best out doors – in the court or on the lawn of some old farm house, for then the eyes of the spectators coming fresh from the light inside take in only an impressionist picture of the scene, and the horse in the dim winter's night, made even more indistinct by occasional cross rays of flickering light from the windows, becomes a monster of weird and awesome possibilities [2], and the stranger to the custom, who sees it thus for the first time, may well feel that he is beholding the mutilated remnant of some pageant of the past – lost to us save so far as these few relics have remained fixed in the traditions of the country side.

Good old hooden horse – the possible frightener of children and to those no longer children the bringer-back of memories of happy frights when once they were. 'Is the hooden horse coming round?' is the first enquiry of the exile on his return home for Christmas after years of absence.

I must now return to description. On Christmas Eve it is difficult to obtain any very definite idea as to the make-up of the horse, but a reference to the photographs will show that it consists of a horse's head crudely carved from a block of wood and painted, the carver evidently being of the conventional school of art. The head is securely fixed to the end of a stout wooden staff about four feet in length. In connection with the head is a piece of stout sacking [3] in the shape of a sack. Under this sack-cloth the hoodener conceals himself, so that only his legs are seen; grasping with his hands the staff to which the head is fixed he stoops down until the staff touches the ground, thus serving as a support. The lower jaw of the head works on a hinge and attached to it is a leather lace or stout cord which the hoodener pulls repeatedly, bringing the lower jaw sharply into contact with the upper jaw, and as both upper and lower jaws are thickly studded with hobnails for teeth, the result is a loud snapping noise supposed to represent the champing of a horse.

In the interests of historical accuracy, I ought to state the time, place and circumstances, under which the accompanying photographs 'A', 'B' and 'C' were taken. I had for some years been wishing to have a group of hoodeners photographed, but the difficulty of doing so at Christmas time – the proper season – was very great. In the early summer of 1905, I chanced to mention the matter to Mr. H. H. Miles, of Millbank, Hoath, and he undertook to get a company together at Sarre. Accordingly, one afternoon, in the beginning of June, 1905, the meeting was arranged there. The company ultimately appeared; they were men employed with the horses on Hale Farm, St. Nicholas-at-Wade. It was past six o'clock, the company had to dress, the weather threatened rain, we were on tenterhooks, as the light was failing. At last they were dressed. Then another hitch arose; Mr. Thomas Champion had allowed us to have the group taken in his yard at Bolingbroke Farm, Sarre, but his stable fittings were up to date in character, and comprised nothing so ancient as a *birch* broom, it was impossible for Mollie to sweep with a bass broom, and consequently in the first photograph 'A' Mollie is shown playing on the triangle. On the extreme left is one of the musicians armed with a tambourine, next comes Mollie, unfortunately without her broom (which was even in course of manufacture), then the Horse with the Rider [4] standing behind, while the Waggoner is holding the halter in his left hand and the whip in his right, the group being completed by the Concertina Player on the extreme right.

Another photograph was taken of the same group as 'A' with the Rider in the act of mounting. As a picture this was a failure, and is not reproduced.

At that time I regarded – though I am now convinced *wrongly* – the presence of the musicians as being a modern importation into the company, and photograph 'B' shows the group without the tambourine and concertina. In the meantime, as will be seen, the birch broom for Mollie had been hastily impromptorised.

It then occurred to us that in taking the right side of the horse the glory of his mane (made of brilliant coloured ribbon, in Kent called 'caytis') and tail had not had justice done them. Accordingly the photograph 'C' was taken, showing the Hoodener out of his disguise and holding up the head. A considerable amount of detail will be noticed. The ears are pointed pieces of leather. The head is decorated with all the trappings usual in the case of a Kent farm horse in that district when dressed in state. On the top of the head, between the ears, with a swinging disc, is the head brass, and on the forehead the circular brass ornament called the face piece.

The working arrangement of the lower jaw is shown, which in the Thanet horse is absurdly short, and one should not overlook the tail, which is made of a small piece of horse-hair decorated with caytis. The bridle is a long piece of leather thickly covered with brass studs.

Mollie, I am informed, is dying out in Thanet, and apparently was revived and brought into the group for my benefit; be that as it may, Mollie invariably accompanied the hoodeners on Christmas Eve, in the years 1888 – 1892, which I spent at Gore Street, Monkton, with my uncle, Mr F. de B. Collard, who lived there at that time.

In Thanet the practice of the custom is almost entirely, if not quite, restricted to the men on the farm who have charge of the farm horses, and formerly, I am told, a farm with more than one team would have a hooden horse to each team; when not in use it is kept in the stable.

Hoodening at Walmer. Shortly before Christmas, 1906, I had a conversation with Mr. Vaughan Page, of Canterbury, as to the observance of the custom at Walmer. He told me that his father (Mr. Henry Page) recollected the custom at Walmer back to, at any rate,

1849, in which year he became tenant of Walmer Court Farm, remaining there until 1896. During this period the men on Walmer Court Farm always went round at Christmas with the hooden horse; the musicians who accompanied them relying to a large extent on sheep-bells – one in each hand. They had no Mollie.

Mr. P. T. Greensted, who succeeded Mr. Page, and was tenant of Walmer Court Farm until 1903, informs me the custom went on during the whole of his time. I subsequently ascertained that the leader at Walmer was Mr. Robert Laming, May's Lane, Walmer.

Accordingly on Christmas Eve, 1906, I went to Walmer, and having ascertained the time when the party would set out, I had a comfortable tea at the hotel near Walmer Station. While at tea, a man in grotesque attire came into the room, and proceeded to blacken his face with burnt cork at the fire. I, who had thoughts for nothing but hoodening, enquired if he were one of *that* party, "No," he said, and it appeared he was one of the Walmer Nigger Minstrels with no very great opinion of such obsolescent customs as hoodening.

However, very shortly afterwards, the well-known clap! clap! was heard from within the bar – the Hoodeners had come. I hastened to see them. The party consisted of four, the hoodener with the horse's head, the man whose duty it is to lead the horse, and when not doing so, to play the triangle, and two musicians, one playing the tambourine and the other the concertina. The wooden head is made on the same lines as the Thanet horse, but it is somewhat larger and the jaws open much further back and therefore wider. Here I found the practice was that the 'gratuity' had to be placed in the horse's jaws, and on this particular occasion the horse put his head on the counter of the bar while the landlord's little daughter was lifted up from the other side in order to carry out the proper form of giving the money, after conquering her fright, real or feigned, she accomplished her task. I had a short conversation with the leader, Mr. Robert Laming, he told me that his horse was not the one which used to belong to the Walmer Court men; he did not know what had become of that, that he had been out with his horse on Christmas Eve for this five and twenty years, and missed doing so only one year. The Walmer party were in their ordinary clothes, but formerly I was told they wore smock frocks. At Walmer they had no Mollie, nor any recollection of her. I accompanied the party a little way on their rounds which I was told would not finish till about 11; it was then 6.30, and I found the hoodeners sure of their welcome, the horse gambolled into all the crowded shops, and at Christmas they are crowded, and everyone was pleased except a collie dog which worked himself into a fearful rage but feared to try his teeth against the wooden jaws of the horse. On visiting the butcher, he, regardless of the graminivorous habits of the animal, placed a mutton chop in the jaws besides the accustomed tribute, a piece of humour which met with great applause.

I had intended to walk on to Deal and look for the hoodening parties there, but the night was so forbidding, that I returned direct to Canterbury, after making an arrangement with Mr. Laming for a meeting some other day to photograph the group. I could not get the party together until 29th March, 1907, when the photographs 'D', 'E' and 'F' were taken at Walmer. The trouble on this occasion was an excess of light, for it was a bright sunny day, and a shady spot was found with difficulty. The photograph 'D' was first taken, on the extreme left is Robert Laming with the concertina, next comes the horse, whose part is taken by Harry Axon; William Laming (Robert's brother) has the triangle, and Joseph Laming (Robert's son) the tambourine. The next photograph 'E' represents the horse rearing, the Walmer horse was very fond of rearing; it is easier to walk in that way than on all fours, especially as the covering does not meet just under the horse's head, affording a convenient peep hole. The third photograph 'F' shows the horse holding his own head, thus dispelling any illusion of reality. An inspection of the photographs of the Walmer group will readily show the slight points of difference between the Walmer and Thanet horses. It will be seen that the Walmer horse has no pretence to tail or mane. The jaws of the Walmer horse, as before stated, open back further, the hinge being much nearer the throat; which is the older type I cannot say. The swinging brass disk which forms the ornament to the head of the Thanet horse gives place in the Walmer horse to three brass bells, showing its place in the team. In addition to these two types of head, I have found a third; the Lower Hadres horse (now lost) is described to me 'as being more like a horse', having a distinct neck.

Having given these descriptions of the custom, I propose in the next chapter to set out what others have said concerning it before proceeding to any discussion.

CHAPTER II

PRINTED REFERENCES TO THE CUSTOM

It was originally my intention to head this Chapter 'Literature', but this is perhaps too pretentious an expression to use in connection with this small subject.

This present book owes its existence entirely to the collection of extracts from various sources which I had made in the hope that by piercing together the different versions some clue might be obtained. I propose now to give in order of date all references in print which I have found on the hooden horse. I am aware that as regards the earlier accounts, founded on the *European Magazine,* this course will necessitate a good deal of, what may be considered, wearisome repetition, and I may be regarded as pedantic, but to explain the differences between the various versions would involve greater length than printing them in full, and I wished to present a complete record.

In a large number of cases, the writers, following one another without any enquiry, regard the custom as dead and proceed to premature burial and the erection of monuments with inadequate epitaphs. I shall, however, in setting out the following extracts confine my comments chiefly to questions of fact, and I must not be considered as agreeing with the inferences and explanations suggested by various writers. These are matters which will be discussed in a later chapter.

The earliest writer who mentions the custom is Dr. Samuel Pegge, and very properly, for he was the father of the study of the Kentish Dialect. Pegge was the Vicar of Godmersham, Kent, from 1731 to 1751. He was a well-known literary man in his day, and an extensive contributor to the *Gentleman's Magazine* in the eighteenth century, where many articles by him are to be found above the signature 'T. Row' and the anagram 'Paul Gemsege'.

Pegge's ALPHABET OF KENTICISMS.

Hooding (huod•ing) a country masquerade at Christmas time, which in Derb. They call *guising* (I suppose a contraction of *dis-guising*), and in other place *mumming.*

The above is extracted from the collection of Kentish words, made by Pegge while Vicar of Godmersham. The M.S. ultimately found itself in the ownership of Sir Frederic Madden, at the sale of his library it was bought by Dr. Skeat, on behalf of the English Dialect Society, by whom it was printed. (Series C., 1876, of the Society's Publications). It is also printed in Arch. Cant., Vol. IX.

EUROPEAN MAGAZINE, vol. 51, p.358. (May, 1807).

To the editor of the *European Magazine*. Sir, Some time since, in a journey through Kent, I saw in Maidstone Churchyard the following curious epitaph:-

Sacred to the Memory of Mr. Robert Nethersole, who left Issue a Third Wife and Two Children.

Also at Ramsgate, in Kent, I found they begin the festivities of Christmas by a curious procession: a party of young people procure the head of a dead horse, which is affixed to a pole about four feet in length; a string is affixed to the lower jaw; a horse-cloth is also attached to the whole, under which one of the party gets, and by frequently pulling the string, keeps up a loud snapping noise, and is accompanied by the rest of the party, grotesquely habited, with hand-bells; they thus proceed from house to house, ringing their bells, and singing carols and songs; they are commonly gratified with beer and cake, or perhaps with money. This is called, *provincially,* a Hodening, and the figure above described a Hoden, or Woden horse. Is the above a relic of a festival to commemorate our Saxon ancestors landing in Thanet, as the term Woden seems to imply? Perhaps some of your readers can clear this up. It is, I find, general in Thanet on Christmas Eve, and, as far as I can learn, nowhere else.

I am, Sir, Your very humble servant and well wisher.

The above extract from the *European Magazine* should be particularly noted, it is the earliest *description* of the custom I have found, and, moreover, this description has been copied almost verbatim by a large number of other works. It will be observed that the writer speaks of the 'head of a *dead* horse' being used, this, of course, is not impossible as a real horse's head is still used, as will be seen, in similar customs on other parts of the country, but the type of head of the hooden horse used at the present day is of such a conventional and archaic type as to render it unlikely that the wooden head is a modern innovation, and I shall be able to show by reliable oral tradition that the wooden head was in use as far back as 1824. The anonymous contributor to the *European Magazine* apparently did not speak from personal knowledge, but from information received, he clearly was not a native of Kent, and therefore I do not think this account is very reliable in matters of detail. The expression 'the figure above described (is called) a hoden or woden horse' goes to show that at that date a wooden horse was used. Neither the number of the party nor their movements merit the term 'procession'.

RELICS FOR THE CURIOUS. In two Vols. Legendary Tales, Singular Customs, &c. London. Printed for Samuel Burton, Leadenhall Street, 1824. Vol. I, p.3.

Going a Hodening. *A curious custom in Kent.* [This version follows that in the *European Magazine* beginning 'At Ramsgate' down to the words 'perhaps with money']; it then concludes with a variation as follows]. This is called *provincially* a Hodening; and the figure above described a Hoden, or Wooden Horse. This curious ceremony is always observed in the Isle of Thanet on Christmas Eve, and is supposed to be an ancient relic of a festival, to commemorate our Saxon ancestors landing in Thanet, as the term Hoden seems to imply.

It will be noted that the expression in the *European Magazine*, 'Hoden or Woden Horse', appears in the last extract as 'Hoden or *Wooden* Horse', and that the supposed connection with our Saxon ancestors, which in the *European Magazine* is put interrogatively, is in this version put affirmatively.

CONCERT ROOM AND ORCHESTRA ANECDOTES OF MUSIC AND MUSICIANS. Ancient and Modern, by Thos. Busby, Mus. D., London, 1825. (Three Vols.) Vol. I, p. 73.

A Hodening.

At Ramsgate, in Kent, they begin the festivities of Christmas by a curious musical procession. A party of young people procure the head of a dead horse, which is affixed to a pole about four feet in length; a string is tied to the lower jaw; a horsecloth is also attached to the whole, under which one of the party gets, and by frequently pulling the string, keeps up a loud snapping noise, and is accompanied by the rest of the party, grotesquely habited, and ringing handbells. They thus proceed from house to house, sounding their bells, and singing carols and songs. They are commonly gratified with beer and cake, or perhaps with money. This is provincially called a Hodening; and the figure above described a Hoden, or Wooden horse. This curious ceremony is also observed in the Isle of Thanet on Christmas Eve; and is supposed to be an ancient relic of a festival, ordained to commemorate our Saxon ancestors landing in that island.

[Index at end of Vol. III has] A*n* Hodening I, 73

It is curious to observe the insertion of the word 'musical', which can only have been done to justify the insertion in a book of anecdotes of *Music,* &c.

Hone's EVERY DAY BOOK (1826). Vol. I, p. 1642.

'HODENING' IN KENT.

[The same version as in Busby's *Concert Room and Orchestra Anecdotes*, to which it is attributed.]

THE MIRROR OF LITERATURE, AMUSEMENT AND INSTRUCTION. London, printed and published by J. Limbird, 143 Strand. Vol. xx (1832), p. 419.

Manners and Customs.
KENT.

At Ramsgate they commence their Christmas festivities by the following ceremony: A party of the youthful portion of the community having procured the head of a horse, it is affixed to a pole, about four feet in length; a string is tied to the lower jaw, a horse cloth is tied round the extreme part of the head, beneath which one of the party is concealed, who, repeated pulling and loosening the string, causes the jaw to rise and fall, and thus produces, by bringing the teeth in contact, a snapping noise, as he moves along; the rest of the party following in procession, grotesquely habited, and ringing hand-bells. In this order they proceed from house to house, singing carols and ringing their bells, and are generally remunerated for the amusement they occasion by a largess of money, or beer and cake. This ceremony is called 'a hoodening'. The figure which we have described is designated 'a hooden' or wooden horse. The ceremony prevails in many parts of the Isle of Thanet, and may probably be traced as the relic of some religious ceremony practised in the early ages by our Saxon ancestors.

THE BOOK OF CHRISTMAS, by Thomas K. Hervey (illustrated by R. Seymour, published by Wm. Spooner, 1836), p.216.

The musical procession, known in the Isle of Thanet, and other part of the same county, by the name of 'hodening', (supposed by some, to be an ancient relic of a festival ordained to commemorate the landing of our Saxon ancestors, in that island, and which, in its form, is neither more nor less than a modification of the old practice of the 'hobby horse') is, to this day, another of the customs of this particular period.

Hervey's *Book of Christmas* is little known now-a-days, but of great interest. It is a small octavo and contains about 30 plates descriptive of Christmas drawn by Seymour, who drew the first two illustrations to Pickwick.

THE GENTLEMAN'S MAGAZINE, January, 1845, 'Minor Correspondence', p.2.

W.J.T. is anxious for information relative to the practice of 'Hodening', or carrying a horse's head in procession, formerly observed in Kent, at Christmas Eve; more particularly, whether the custom still exists, &c.

This query appears never to have had any reply in the *Gentleman's Magazine*, but it is referred to in Dunkin's *History of Kent.*

Brand's POPULAR ANTIQUITIES, Bohn's Edition, 3 Vols., 1849. Vol. I, p.474.

Going A Hodening.

At Ramsgate, in Kent, they commenced the festivities of Christmas by a curious procession. A party of young people procured the head of a dead horse, which is affixed to a pole about four feet in length; a string was affixed to the lower jaw; a horsecloth was also attached to the whole, under which one of the party got, and by frequently pulling the string, kept up a loud snapping noise, and was accompanied by the rest of the party, grotesquely habited, with handbells. They thus proceeded from house to house, ringing their bells, and singing carols and songs. They are commonly offered refreshments or money. This was provincially called a hodening, and the figure above described a hoden or wooden horse. It is now discontinued, but the singing of carols at Christmas is still called *hodening*.

It will be seen that the last extract is almost verbatim the same as that in Busby's *Concert Room Anecdotes*, &c., and in Hone's *Every Day Book*, except that the past tense is used instead of the present.

Halliwell's DICTIONARY OF ARCHAIC AND PROVINCIAL WORDS. *1852.*

HODENING. A custom formerly prevalent in Kent at Christmas Eve, when a horse's head was carried in procession. This is now discontinued, but the singing of carols at that season is still called *hodening*.

Dunkin's HISTORY OF KENT (*1856*).

HODENING. In the Gentleman's Magazine for January, 1845, it is stated that formerly there was a practice observed in Kent of 'Hodening', or carrying a horse's head in procession at Christmas Eve. Now this word, most probably is a corruption and means 'Hobening'.

Jabez Allies in his tract on 'The Ignis Fatuus or Will o' the Wisp and the Fairies' says that the words hoberdy, hobany, and hob, most probably like the word hobby, are all derived from the Gothic word 'hoppe', which signifies a horse, for we find that in various legends, relative to sprites, &c., fiend horses form a prominent part, and as the movements of the ignes fatui resemble in a measure the cantering motion of a horse that may have been the reason why the names in question were given to these interesting meteors; and here we appear to have the true meaning of the word hobgoblin, that is a fiend horse.

Kentish Proverb 'My legs be as big as hobble postis',

and hence the words hobby horse, and hobble. A light kind of horsemen who were stationed in particular places to give notice of the approach of an enemy in the day time were ancient called 'Hobelers'.

The watch set at *la Zenlade* in the hundred of Hoo, in this county, consisted of twelve men at arms and six hobelers. The Textus Roffensis, ap.Hasted, says they rode about from 'place to place in the night'. We have the word 'hobble' used in Kent for fastening the forefeet of horses closely together, to prevent them straying when turned out upon the commons, or 'the long acre', i.e., the strip of green in country lanes. A hobbling or awkward gaited country lad is called a hoberdy hoy.

It is evident the writer was not acquainted with the actual pronunciation, for apparently he thought that the first vowel was short and that hooden or hoden rhymed with sodden. I think that the derivation given in the above extract may be ignored.

Thomas Wright's DICTIONARY OF OBSOLETE AND PROVINCIAL ENGLISH, *(Bohn)* 1857

HODENING, s. An old custom in Kent, on Christmas Eve, when a horse's head was carried in procession; it is now discontinued, but the singing of carols is still called *hodening.*

GUIDE TO THE COAST OF KENT, *by Walcott, published by Edward Stanford, 1859, p.110.*

[RAMSGATE.] A curious custom used to prevail called 'going a hodening', which consisted in singing carols, while a horse's head (hoden) carved in wood was carried in procession; to the songs were added the ringing of hand-bells, and the snapping of the jaws of the hobby.

This appears to be the first printed reference in which the horse's head is stated to be carved of wood.

NOTES AND QUERIES, *Series II, vol. 8, p.486. December 17th, 1859.*

How many quaint and apparently unmeaning customs exist, or have existed lately, in various parts of the country, on which, obscure as they may at first sight seem, some light may be thrown by research among the traditions of the neighbourhood, or the labours of Continental Antiquaries.

Gay's Epilogue to *The What d'ye call it,*

> 'Our Stage Play has a moral, and no doubt
> You all have sense enough to find it out'.

might well be parodied, with reference to such enquiries, after this fashion:-

> 'Each custom has its meaning, there's no doubt,
> Had we but sense enough to find it out'.

For instance, the Kentish custom of Hodening:- [Here follows verbatim the version from Busby and Hone before quoted.]

This is told by Busby in his *Court Room Anecdotes*, thence transferred to Hone's *Every Day Book* (II, 1642). From Hone it finds its way into Brand's great storehouse of *Popular Antiquities* (I, 474, ed. 1849), and there it is left; but who can doubt that if any zealous member of the Kentish Archaeological Society would look into the *Deutsche Mythologie* of that most profound scholar Jacob Grimm, he would find something new and worth telling in illustration of the very curious custom? AMBROSE MERTON.

This challenge to the Kent Archaeological Society seems never to have been accepted. Grimm will be referred to later on this book. 'Ambrose Merton' was the pseudonym of William John Thoms, the founder and first Editor of *Notes and Queries*.

ONCE A WEEK, Vol. VI, December 28th, 1861, p.25. 'Christmas and how it was kept' at p.26.

On Christmas Eve, at Ramsgate and in the Isle of Thanet, the young men, grotesquely habited, come 'a hodening', i.e., carrying a dead horse's head upon a pole four feet long, snapping the jaws of the hoden or horse together by pulling a string, while their mates ring hand-bells and sing carols.

This passage is re-printed verbatim in the issue of the *Kent Herald* for January 2nd, 1862, p.3, col. 2, except that 'a horse's head' is spoken of, and not 'a *dead* horse's head'.

THANET ADVERTISER, December 31st, 1864, p.3, col. 3.

MINSTER. The great festival of Christmas has been kept here as heretofore. On Christmas Eve we had the merry old Church bells pealing forth the glad tidings. The band enlivened the streets; hooded horses not hooded quite up to the old style, perambulated the streets, and the carol singers, some *in* tune and others *out* of tune, were very numerous.

This is the first original reference to the custom which I have been able to find in the local newspapers.

KENTISH GAZETTE, January 7th, 1868, p.4, col. 6.

KENT HERALD, January 9th, 1868, p.3.

MINSTER. * * * Christmas has been, and gone again, with its varied pleasures and happy meetings. Our merry old Church bells, which have probably never failed to give out the good tidings since their tongues were placed in them, about the year 1620, that Christmas was at hand, have not failed in pouring forth their homely sounds, only appreciated by sensitive minds. Hoodening was also the order of the evening on Christmas Eve, and although there are but a few things without exceptions, we fear carolling does not improve, and the jingling noise called hand-bell ringing was fearful. The hooden horse, we thought, was as extinct as the megatharium, but there was one that came again to see how the world was jogging on. The darkies performed their part very well, and one or two sets of carol singers put one in mind of the days of yore. * * *

Brand's POPULAR ANTIQUITIES, edited by Hazlitt (J. R. Smith, 1870), vol. I, p.149.

It has been satisfactorily shown that the *Mari Lhoyd* [sic], or horse's skull decked with ribbons, which used to be carried about at Christmas in Wales, was not exclusively a Welsh custom, but was known and practised in the Border-counties. It was undoubtedly a form of the Old English Hobby Horse.

Ibid. p.288.

HODENING. Mr Busby in his *Concert Room Anecdotes*, who is followed by Hone and Ambrose Merton (in 'Notes and Queries' for Dec. 17, 1859), or rather reprinted by them, gives an account of this usage, which is merely another form of the 'Mari Llwyd' already described.

The first quotation is necessary to explain the second. The statements that the Mari Llwyd is undoubtedly a form of the old English Hobby Horse, and that Hodening is merely another form of the Mari Llwyd, must not be too lightly accepted, in the Mari Llwyd a real horse's skull is used. See Chapter IV.

A BOOK OF THE BEGINNINGS, by Gerald Massey. Williams and Norgate (1881). Vol. I, p.300-1.

Not long ago the festivities of Christmas commenced at Ramsgate, Kent, with a strange procession, in front of which was carried the head of a dead horse, affixed to a pole four feet long; a string was attached to the lower jaw and pulled frequently, so that the head kept snapping with a loud noise. The people who accompanied the horse's head were grotesquely habited, and carried hand-bells; the procession went from house to house with the bells ringing and the jaws snapping, and this was called a-Hodening.

Our word head is the Egyptian Hut, head, and height. Hutr (*Eg.*) is the going horse. The winged Hut was the symbol of the sun, and the horse was also adopted as a type of the swift goer. Hutu (*Eg.*) means one half or half way round the circle. One Huti image is the demoniacal head on a staff, the ideograph of throat and swallowing. The action of the horse jaws suggests that of swallowing. Huter is a ring, and they made the ring in going round a hodening. The Hut (*Eg.*) is the good demon. And the horse head was typical of the Hut and of the horse constellation, Pegasus, which the sun at one time entered at the turn of the winter solstice some five thousand years ago. Uttara-Bhadrapada is the twenty-seventh lunar mansion in the Hindu asterisms, partly in Pegasus. This was the point at which the sun began to mount, hence the winged horse.

The horse head was the Hut (Hutr), the good demon threatening and terrifying and overcoming the powers of darkness. The horse was a substitute for the ass of Sut-Typhon, which was condemned at a very early period in Egypt, so early as to be almost absent from the monuments except as the symbol of Typhon.

If for a moment we restore the ass, then this 'hodening', with the horse's head and snapping jaws is the exact replica of the jaw bone of the ass with which the Jewish solar hero slew the Philistines. The Hebrew mythology made use of the ass instead of the horse; the ass on which the Shiloh rode, the Shiloh being the young hero, the avenger of his father, in the Hebrew myth Shem-son. The singing of carols at Christmas is still called hodening.

Our old friend, the *European Magazine* version revived again, but in what a strange oriental trappings disguised – a mixture of 'She' and 'the Light of Asia'. What is to be made of the above extract? One does not so much object to the attempt to solar-mythise the hooden horse, it was inevitable that this should be done by someone, at some time or other, but one does resent the attempt to do so, via the story of Samson and the jaw-bone of the ass.

Parish & Shaw's DICTIONARY OF THE KENTISH DIALECT (1888).

HODENING (hod•ning) *partc.* A custom formerly prevalent in Kent on Christmas Eve; it is now discontinued, but the singing of carols at that season is still called *hodening*. (See *Hoodening*).

HOODENING (huod•ning) *sb.* The name formerly given to a mumming or masquerade. Carol singing, on Christmas Eve, is still so called at Monckton [sic], in East Kent.

The late Rev. H. Bennett Smith, Vicar of St. Nicholas-at-Wade, the adjoining parish to Monckton, wrote as follows in 1876, – 'I made enquiry of an old retired farmer in my parish, as to the custom called *Hoodning*. He tells me that formerly the farmer used to send annually round the neighbourhood the best horse under the charge of the wagoner, and that afterwards instead, a man used to represent the horse, being supplied with a tail, and with a wooden [pronounced ooden or hooden] figure if a horse's head, and plenty of horse hair for a mane. The horse's head was fitted with hobnails for teeth; the mouth being made to open by means of a string, and in closing made a loud crack. The custom has long since ceased'.

Sometimes it is difficult to comment on inaccuracies in a courteous manner. There *is* a hooden horse at St. Nicholas-at-Wade to this present day, it went round this very last Christmas (1908), and there is ample evidence that the custom has been regularly carried on in that district as far back as living memory goes. I have spoken to men who can speak from personal knowledge of the early forties of the last century and of tradition behind that. I saw it myself, at Monkton, the very year that the Dictionary was published. Perhaps the 'Old Retired Farmer' was a curmudgeon (though there are not many in the Island) and the hoodeners may have feared a pail of cold water from the first floor window in return for their performance, instead of the customary oblation, and on that account they may never have visited him. His explanation of the origin of the custom may be dismissed as sheer guesswork. One might be led to suppose, from the Dictionary, that there were two distinct customs, 'hodening' and 'hoodening', and certainly that the pronunciation of each of these words was different, but neither of these suppositions is correct. There is *one* custom, the name of which is spelt in either of the two ways, and the pronunciation of both spellings is alike.

THE KENTISH NOTE BOOK (edited by George O. Howell), vol. i, p.19, December 22nd, 1888.

Going a-Hodening.

The following account of a curious Christmas custom, that used to prevail in the Isle of Thanet, is taken from a book entitled *Relics for the Curious*, published in 1824. [Here follows verbatim the before quoted extract from *Relics for the Curious* down to, and including, the words 'This curious ceremony is always observed in the Isle of Thanet on Christmas Eve', the remainder of the passage being left out]. From enquiries I find that this old custom has died out, at least in Ramsgate. As will be observed, mention is made of hand-bell ringing in these grotesque processions, and it is interesting to note that, to this day, there are several families residing in Ramsgate who are clever hand-bell ringers, and who have been so for some generations back. INVICTA.

THE BROMLEY RECORD, No. 377, December 1st, 1889, p. 190, col. 2.

At Ramsgate the Christmas festivities were formerly commenced by a curious musical procession, known as hodening. A party of young people procure the head of a dead horse, which was affixed to a pole about four feet in length, a string was tied to the lower jaw, and a horse cloth was attached to the whole, under which one of the party got, and by frequent pulling the string kept up a loud snapping noise, and was accompanied by the rest of the party grotesquely habited and ringing hand-bells. They thus proceeded from house to house, sounding bells and singing carols and songs as they went. This quaint custom is said sometimes to have been kept up on Christmas Eve, but it is now entirely discontinued.

Ibid. (No. 378), January 1st, 1890, p. 15, col. I [Reprinted in Howell's *Kentish Note Book*, vol. I, p. 320, April 26th, 1890].

An Old Custom.

To the Editor of 'The Bromley Record' Sir, In your issue for December I notice an allusion to the ancient custom of 'Hodening' at Ramsgate on Christmas Eve.

During my residence in the Isle of Thanet for some years, I have frequently conversed with old residents on the subject, and gather from them that the custom was discontinued some fifty years since, in consequence of a woman at Broadstairs being so scared by it that her death resulted. I cannot find that it was practised at all beyond the Isle of Thanet, so conclude that it was peculiar to this portion of the county of Kent. A natural horse's head was rarely hired owing to the difficulty procuring one, but one carved from wood block was generally used as a substitute. The Company consisted of a man carrying the horse's head upon a short pole, and attired as you describe, one called the 'Jockey', one dressed as, and called the 'old woman', with a broom, two singers, and two stalwart attendants, who were useful in the case of a 'row'. The 'Jockey' placed himself upon the back of the man carrying the horse's head, and it was the 'sport' of the bystanders to remove him, if possible, from his mount. This led to some rough play, and it was frequently necessary to call the services of the 'stalwarts' into requisition. Many a bloody battle, they tell me, has been fought at a 'Hodening'. The 'old woman' swept with the broom the feet of those who answered the knock at the door, and well chasing the girls was only induced to desist by a gift of money or refreshments. The singers indulged the whole time, in carols formerly, but in combination of carols and song latterly.

In Hone's *Every Day Book*, published in 1827, is mentioned the custom as appertaining to Ramsgate chiefly, but also in the Isle of Thanet. All the neighbouring villages, St. Peter's, St. Lawrence, Minster, St. Nicholas, Acol, Monkton, and Birchington, I find observed it, but an old resident informed me that Minster was the 'headest and toppingest' for it. He said that after the

Magistrates cried it down, they were afraid to go out with the 'hodenhouse' [sic] for fear they should fall into the hands of the 'patrols' and bosholders'. These were the officers of the 'Court Leet', and probably acted as Assistant Constables. * * *You are quite at liberty to insert this letter if the above facts would interest your readers. I am, Sir, Yours obediently, CHARLES J. H. SAUNDERS. St. Lawrence, Thanet, December 16th, 1889.

The statement that 'the custom was discontinued fifty years since' may be true as regards *St. Lawrence.*

THE CHURCH TIMES, *December 24th, 1890, p.1270, col. 2 (Peter Lombard's Varia Column).*

Hone says that in the Isle of Thanet it is the custom on Christmas Eve to get the head of a horse, fix it on a pole, and hang a horse cloth below. This pole is then carried by one of the party, who by means of a string attached to the lower jaw, keeps up a snapping noise; the rest of his companions, grotesquely habited, ring bells and sing carols. This, he says, is called 'Hodening', and is supposed to be an ancient relic of a festival ordered to commemorate the coming of the English to the island, bearing a white horse as their standard, in 449. I fear this custom, too, has passed away like the Old Style. I once lived for a few years in Thanet and never heard of it.

Ibid. January 2nd, 1891, p.20, col. I.

Two pleasant letters from East Kent inform me that 'Hodening' still goes on, not indeed in Thanet, but at Deal and Walmer. This is from a parson's wife:- 'When we lived at Deal, our children used to be half frightened and half amused by a performance which took place annually on the day you mention. We were warned of the arrival of this creature by a very loud clapping noise, and on rushing to the street door, saw a horse's head, supported on a pole by a man in a crawling position so as to resemble an animal, and covered in front by a coarse cloth. Nothing was done or sung by the small crowd around; and the clapping caused by the opening and shutting of the mouth continued, till the creature having been satisfied with money was driven away. Do you think it may be a remnant of the old Teutonic sacrifices of horses mentioned in Scheffel's 'Ekkehard', which Audifax and Hadumoth see without being observed, and about which 'Ekkehard' questions the Waldfrau'. [5]

Ibid. January 9th, 1891, p.31, col. 2.

I have to confess, with sincere regret, a piece of carelessness, and to ask the forbearance of three correspondents. Going to the post office down in the country, I received and opened a parcel of letters from the Editor of this paper, among them some very interesting communications concerning 'Hodening' and other folklore. And I have lost them and I don't know how! I was rather trussed up on account of the cold, and I suppose must have missed my pocket. One was from Huddersfield, another from Cheshire. Will my kind correspondents show that they have forgiven me by writing again?

Ibid. January 23rd, 1891, p.78.

Hearty thanks to the friends who have written to me again. I cannot, of course, be sure that all have done so, whose letters I lost, but I think they have. 'Hodening' claims first place. 'It was observed on Christmas Eve at Walmer in 1886, which was the last time I spent the festival there,' writes one antiquary. Another writes: 'When I was a lad, about 45 years since, it was always the custom on Christmas Eve with the male farm-servants from every farm in our parish of Hoath (Borough of Reculver) and neighbouring parishes of Herne and Chislet, to go round in the evening from house to house with the Hoodining Horse, which consisted of the imitation of a horse's head made of wood, life-size, fixed on a stick about the length of a broom handle: the lower jaw of the head was made to open with hinges, a hole was made through the roof of the mouth, then another through the forehead coming out by the throat, through this was passed a cord attached to the lower jaw, which when pulled by the cord at the throat caused it to close and open; on the lower jaw large headed hob-nails were driven in to form the teeth. The strongest of the lads was selected for the horse; he stooped and made as long a back as he could, supporting himself with the stick carrying the head; then he was covered with a horse cloth, and one of his companions mounted his back. The horse had a bridle and reins. Then commenced the kicking, rearing, jumping, &c., &c., and the banging together of the teeth. As soon as the doors were opened the 'horse' would pull his string incessantly, and the noise made can be better imagined than described. I confess that in my very young days I was horrified at the approach of the hoodining horse, but as I grew older I used to go round with them. I was at Hoath on Thursday last, and asked if the custom was still kept up. It appears it is now three or four years since it has taken place. I never heard of it in the Isle of Thanet. There was no singing going on with the hoodining horse, and the party was strictly confined to the young men who went with the horses on the farms. I have seen some of the wooden heads carved out quite hollow in the throat part, and two holes bored through the forehead to form the eyes. The lad who played the horse would hold a lighted candle in the hollow, and you can imagine how horrible it was to one who opened the door to see such a thing close to his eyes. Carollers in those days were called hoodiners in the parishes I have named'.

And the following communication is interesting and valuable:-

'Some such custom prevailed in the 7th century. In the Penitential of Archbishop Theodore (d. 690) penances are ordained for 'any who on the kalends of January clothe themselves with the skins of cattle and carry heads of animals'. The practice is condemned as being 'dæmoniacum' (See Kemble's *Saxons*, vol. I, p.525). The custom would, therefore, seem to be of pagan origin, and the date is practically synchronous with Christmas, when, according to the rites of Scandinavian mythology, one of the three great annual festivals commenced. At the sacrifices which formed part of these festivals the horse was a frequent victim in the offerings to Odin for martial success, just as in the offerings to Frey for a fruitful year the hog was the chosen animal. I venture, therefore, to suggest that *hodening* (or probably *'Odening*) is a relic of the Scandinavian mythology of our fore-fathers.

[Then follows a reference to the Cheshire custom of Souling].

The account of the custom at Hoath is evidently written by one who knew his subject from personal knowledge.

Ibid. February 6th, 1891, p.125, col. 2.

An esteemed correspondent sends me some very remarkable notes about the horse's head customs, which I must repeat at length. First he quotes three passages from the second volume of Andrew Lang's 'Myth Ritual and Religion'. (1) It is a common ritual custom for the sacrificer to cover himself with the skin and head of the animal sacrificed. In Mexico we know that the Aztec priests wore the flayed skins of their human victims. Lucian gives an instance in his treatise 'De Dea Syria': 'When a man means to go on pilgrimage to Hierapolis he sacrifices a sheep, and eats of its flesh. He then kneels down, and draws the head over his own head, praying at the same time to 'the god'. Chaldean works of art often represent the priest in the skin of the god, sometimes in that of a fish. It is a conjecture not unworthy of consideration that the human gods with bestial heads are derived from the aspect of the celebrant clad in the pelt of the beast whom he sacrifices. In Egyptian art the heads of the gods are usually like masks, or flayed skins, superimposed on the head of a man'. (2) 'A common rite in the dances of totemistic peoples is where the worshippers clothe themselves in the skin of the animals whose feast they celebrate'. (3) 'Certain Californian tribes which worship the buzzard sacrifice him, 'himself to himself' once a year, and use his skin as a covering in the ritual'.

If the horse, says the correspondent, was sacred to Odin, the horse may have been sacrificed to Odin, himself to himself, and the head and skin used in the ritual. Whether hodening and the use of the horse's head is an unconscious confirmation of some heathen tradition or a Christian mockery or parody of it (which the open and unceremonious character described in your notes seems to suggest) there can be little doubt that the explanation is to be sought in the old heathenism of our forefathers. The quotation from Archbishop Theodore's Penitential seems particularly apposite. I daresay Mr. Lang would be glad to know of these old customs, as he has evidently collected very widely in this line.

Those who have not easy access to files of *The Church Times*, will find it convenient to know that a large portion of the above extracts from that paper are quoted in full in Howell's *Kentish Note Book*, Vol. II (published 1894), pp.19 and 22, also in *A Righte Merrie Christmasse*, by John Ashton, published by the Leadenhall Press, pp.114 and 115, and in Walsh's *Curiosities of Popular Customs*, Gibbins & Co., 1898, pp.534-536. *The Church Times* for January 30th and February 20th, 1891, has accounts of other customs which are compared with hoodening.

NOTES AND QUERIES, March 7th, 1891 (7th Series, vol. xi) p.184.

Hodening. The following is a cutting from *The Church Times* of January 23rd. Perhaps some of your readers may be able to supply an account of the origin of this curious custom. [Here follows a reprint of the passage from *The Church Times* of January 23rd, 1891]. E. LEATON-BLENKINSOPP.

Ibid. March 28th, 1891 (7th Series, vol. xi), p.254.

Hodening. Surely this custom of 'hodening' with the 'hoodining horse' is but a remembrance of 'the comming into the hall of the hobby horse' at Christmas. The hobby horse was made much in the same way as the cutting from *The Church Times* describes the 'hoodining' horse to have been, and there can be little doubt they are one and the same. Brand, in his 'Observations' (p.263), says the hobby-horse dance was so called because 'one of the performers carried between his legs the image of a horse made of thin boards'. At Christmas, New Year's Day, and Twelfth Day, lads with these horses, used to go round soliciting alms. J. W. ALLISON. Stratford, E.

This custom is described by Hone (*'Every Day Book'* II, 821, under date December 24), from Busby's *Concert Room and Orchestra Anecdotes*, and, is supposed to be an ancient relic of a festival ordained to commemorate our Saxon ancestors' landing in that island [Thanet]'. H. SCHERREN.

Ibid. May 23rd, 189 I (7th Series, vol. xi), p.415.

Hodening. Irish customs would seem to embrace something similar to the 'hodening' of your correspondents. 'Charlotte Elizabeth', in her interesting *Personal Recollections* (pp.113-14) describes a celebration she witnessed in King's County, 'on that great festival of the peasantry, St. John's Eve'. First on the programme came a huge bonfire on the lawn, followed by promiscuous dancing to the energetic strains of an old blind piper.

'But something was to follow that puzzled me not a little. When the fire had burned for some hours, and got low, an indispensable part of the ceremony commenced. Every one present, of the peasantry, passed through it, and several children were thrown across the sparkling embers, while a wooden frame of some eight feet long, with a horse's head fixed to one end, and a large white sheet thrown over it, concealing the wood and the man on whose head it was carried, made an appearance. This was greeted with loud shouts as the 'white horse'; and having been safely carried by the skill of its bearer several times through the fire with a bold leap. it pursued the people, who ran screaming and laughing in every direction. I asked what the horse was meant for, and was told it represented all cattle. Here was the old worship of Baal, if not of Moloch too, carried on openly and universally in the heart of a nominally Christian country, and by millions professing the Christian name. I was confounded, for I did not then know that Popery is only a crafty adaptation of pagan idolatries to its own scheme; and while I looked upon the now wildly excited people, with their children, and, in a figure, all their cattle, passing again and again through the fire, I almost questioned, in my own mind, the lawfulness of the spectacle'. C. K., Torquay.

Ibid. December 24th, 1892 (8th Series, vol. II), p.505.

Christmas Processions. The following communication occurs in the *Sporting Magazine* for December, 1807. It is signed 'J. J. B.'. It would be well to reproduce it in 'N. and Q.'.

[Here follows the version from the *European Magazlne,* May, 1807, commencing 'At Ramsgate they begin' and ending 'nowhere else'].

The following is extracted from one of the series of articles on Kentish matters which Mr. Alfred Moore, of Eythorne, contributed some years ago to the *Kentish Express* Newspaper, under the title of 'Kentish Odds and Ends'.

'I suppose almost every native of this county has heard the old Kentish word 'hoodenin' and knows the sense in which it is used to-day. But as a good many who are not of Kentish birth are kind enough to read these papers, I may as well say that the word means going round singing carols or songs, or shouting good wishes at Christmas and New Year's Tide, for a consideration, of course, though I hope *that* does not necessarily make them the less kindly meant. Formerly, however, the word had a somewhat different meaning, for a century or so ago it was used for Yuletide mumming or masquerading rather than carol-singing. In East Kent it was then an annual custom for each farmer to send his best horse round the parish in which he lived. Its tail and mane were always gaily decorated, and the animal was in charge of the waggoner, to whom drink and money were given as New Year's perquisites. Sometimes, too, the farm labourers would take *their* 'horse' around, this latter being a rudely cut wooden (pronounced 'ooden' or 'hooden' by the older Kentish folk) figure of a horse's head with moveable mouth, having rows of hobnails for teeth, which, opening and shutting by means of a spring, closed with a loud, sharp snap. It was furnished with a flowing mane and the whole arrangement was worn upon the head of a ploughman, who, supplied with an ample tail to represent the equine caudal appendage, was called the 'hoodener', while his house-to-house visitation of the parish was known as 'hoodenin'. And to-day, although the horse-head mumming custom is forgotten, the old word is still used by us Kentish folks, with an altered meaning, certainly, yet (like almost every vocable in our fine old dialect) carrying us back to bygone days and linking us indissolubly with the Kent of olden times. I have just had a visit from some lads who tell me they are 'out hoodenin' and who have shouted loudly:

> 'We wish ye a murry Chris'mus
> An' a 'appy New Year,
> A pocketful ú money, an'
> A cellarful ú beer.'

Mr. Alfred Moore again referred to the subject when writing on quite a different custom – that of 'going goodenin' on St. Thomas' Day.

Ibid. April 6th, 1895.

After careful investigation and much thought about the matter I incline to the opinion that in both 'Hoodenin' (described by me in the *Kentish Express* of January 5th, 1895) and 'Goodenin', we have preserved the name of the god Woden (or Odin) of our heathen fore-fathers. In the former word the 'h' is generally written but is *never* sounded, while in the latter I cannot help thinking that the 'g' is a later addition to the original form of the word, which, I cannot help thinking was 'Odinin' (or some such form) in both instances. Woden or Odin was one of the old Teutonic and Scandinavian divinities commemorated at the great annual winter festival of Jól, which, commencing at the 'turn of the days' would exactly coincide in point of time with the day which the Christian Church has dedicated to the memory of the doubting Apostle. At this great Jól festival gifts were lavishly bestowed for the glory of the gods of the Teutonic cult and a revel held in their honour, so that *goodenin'* and *hoodenin'* (i.e. winter mumming) were both included in it, and the god Woden being regarded as the ancestor of the Early English chiefs and heroes, he was peculiarly the tutelary divinity of our heathen forefathers and so, as it seems to me, there is small cause for wonder if his name has been perpetuated in Yuletide rites.

Mr. Moore, it is evident, was not personally acquainted with the custom or he would not have said 'the horse mumming custom is forgotten', 'a century or so ago it was used', &c. He appears to have based his remarks on the Old Retired Farmer's inaccuracies which I have already discussed. If Mr. Moore had had any idea that the custom was still practised, I have no doubt that he would have investigated the subject. Mr. Moore's derivation of the word will be considered later.

I find that Christmas carol singing without the hooden horse is still known as 'hoodening' at Ash-next-Sandwich, but it would not be correct to suppose as one might from Mr. Moore, following Parish & Shaw, that 'hoodening' is used generally in Kent to mean carol singing.

OLD ENGLISH CUSTOMS EXTANT AT THE PRESENT TIME. By P. H. Ditchfield, 1896, p.27.

Hoodening is a kind of old horse-head mumming once prevalent in Kent, and still exists in some places. Hoodening is observed still at Walmer; the young men perambulate the village, bearing a Hoodening Horse, a rudely cut wooden figure of a horse's head with movable mouth, having rows of hob-nails for teeth, which opens and shuts by means of a string and closes with a loud sharp snap. It is furnished with a flowing mane, and is worn on the head of a ploughman, who is called the Hoodener. It is suggested that the wooden (pronounced 'ooden or hooden) horse's head gave the name to hoodening or goodening. We must leave the solution of this difficult derivation to the discretion and judgment of our learned readers. *(Footnote* – Hone suggests that it is an ancient relic of a festival ordained to commemorate our Saxon ancestors' landing in the Isle of Thanet). It is evidently connected with the old Pagan feast held on the Kalends of January in the seventh century, when men used to clothe themselves with the skins of cattle and carry heads of animals. A similar custom prevails at Northwich, Cheshire, on All Souls' Day, when a gang of boys and girls come round at night, reciting verses and singing snatches of songs, accompanied by a man dressed as a horse. The monster prances and clatters with its hoofs when a modest coin is presented to it. Possibly hoodening is a relic of the old hobby-horse dance which once formed one of the leading festivities in the Squire's hall at Christmas. At any rate, hoodening is a very ancient custom, which still lingers amongst us, and attracts the attention of the curious in Old English manners.

LAYS AND LEGENDS OF THE WEALD OF KENT, by Lilian Winser (London, Elkin Mathews, 1897), p.4.

> Both o' them sillies heads a band for carrolin' and such,
> And goes, a-hoodenin' for pence, but there, they don't get much!

Only poetic licence can justify the introduction of hoodening into *Lays and Legends* dealing with the Weald of Kent. An explanation of the custom appears on page 75, but as this is evidently founded on the Old Retired Farmer, I have not transcribed it.

THE MAGIC OF THE HORSESHOE. By R. M. Lawrence. (London: Gay & Bird, 1898), pp.84 – 85.

The Christmas festivities at Ramsgate, in Kent, formerly included a peculiar feature called 'going a-hodening'. A horse's head fixed on a pole was carried through the town by a party of young people, grotesquely attired and ringing hand-bells. By pulling a string attached to the lower jaw, the horse's mouth was made to open and shut with a snapping sound. In this case the horse's head was typical of the good Demon, threatening and overcoming the powers of darkness. *(Footnote* – Gerald Massey. *A Book of Beginnings).*

ENGLISH DIALECT DICTIONARY, 1902. Vol. III.

Hoodening, see Hodening.

Hodening, sb. Ken. Also in forms 'hoodening' Ken.,[1] 'hood-ing' Ken.[2] The name formerly given to a mumming or masquerade on Christmas Eve, still applied to the singing of carols.
[Here follow extracts from *Church Times,* January 2nd, 1891. p.20, col. 1; Brand's *Pop. Antiq.,* ed. 1848, vol. I, p.474; Ken.[1] (i.e. Parish & Shaw's *Dictionary of the Kentish Dialect)*; and Ken.[2] (i.e. Pegge's *Glossary)*].

(The word *hoodening* is locally associated with *wooden,* from the wooden figure of the horse's head).

THE TREASURY, January, 1907, 'Winter Customs,' P. H. Ditchfield.

'Hoodening', a kind of old horse head mumming, still exists in some parts of Kent. The young men perambulate the village bearing a Hoodening Horse, a rudely cut figure of a horse's head with a moveable mouth, having rows of hobnails for teeth, which opens and shuts by means of a string, and closes with a loud sharp snap. It is furnished with a flowing mane, and is worn on the head of a ploughman who is called the Hoodman. Various explanations of the origin of the custom have been given. It is probably a relic or the old hobby horse dance, which once formed one of the leading amusements in the squire's hall at Christmas.

This last quotation is almost a verbatim extract from the same writer's *Old English Customs.* The man with the head is called the 'Hoodener' not the Hoodman.

HEALTH RESORT, January, 1907. 'Common Objects of the Seashore at Ramsgate', by J. Harris Stone, M.A., p.20.

A curious old Christmas custom used to be associated with Ramsgate, which is not generally known. I came across it in the *European Magazine for* May, 1907. [Here follows the transcript from the *European Magazine beginning* with 'a party of young people' down to 'a Hoden or Woden Horse'.]

And then this old anthropologist goes on to enquire: 'Is the above a relic of a festival to commemorate our Saxon ancestors landing in Thanet, as the term Woden seems to imply? Perhaps some of your readers can clear this up. It is, I find, general in Thanet on Christmas Eve, and, as far as I can learn, nowhere else'.

It would be interesting to know if this custom or any vestige of it, remains after this hundred years when it was thus observed and noted. Perhaps some of *our* readers, in 1907, may be able to inform us.

Ibid. February, 1907, p.54.

Hodening. The remarks about Hodening, in the article we published last month on Ramsgate, have elicited several interesting replies. The Rev. Chas. W. Whistler, M.R.C.S., of Stockland, Bridgwater, writes:- 'The Ramsgate 'Hodening' is not new to me, and is noticed by the Rev. P. H. Ditchfield, in an article in *The Treasury* for this January, where he says that the custom still exists in some parts or Kent, and suggests that the horse's head may be a survival of the old 'hobby horse', which figured in the mediæval Morris dances. The name of the custom and its association with Christmas would date its origin to still earlier times, however; and there can be little doubt that it is a survival of some Odinic Yuletide solemnity connected with the sacrifice of the horse to the Asir. The victim was usually beheaded, and its flesh was afterwards feasted on, whence probably our objection to the eating of horseflesh, as forbidden to the first Christians from among our Saxon ancestors. 'Hodening' or 'Hoodening' is an intermediate variant of the name of Woden or Odin, which is probably Jutish, though there is a Saxon (not Anglian) tendency to pronounce an initial W as an aspirate, e.g., 'William' as 'Hoolliam'. That this strange custom should, so far as I know, occur only in Jutish Kent (the scene of the earliest landings of our forefathers) is significant, and may indicate that it is a tradition of some very marked sacrifice to the Asir by the first actual intending settlers on their arrival. Dr. Ditchfield adds that the man who carries the horse's head is called the 'Hoodman',[6] and I feel sure that this name may be referred also to Odin, who rides hooded'.

Mr. Alfred Toft, of the 'Crown' Inn, Sarre, Thanet, writes:- 'I have read your very interesting article on 'Common Objects of the Seashore at Ramsgate'. With regard to your allusion to the old Christmas custom of Hodening, I am able to inform you that it is still carried out in its entirety at this old-world village of Sarre. I had several visitors from London staying here last Christmas, and very much to their surprise and amusement the 'Hodeners' made their appearance, and regaled us with a selection of old country songs. The general 'get-up' of the troupe was much as you have described'.

'Ancient One' writes:- 'In *Notes and Quenes,* vol. I, p.173, it is said that this curious custom [7] is prevalent in Wales, namely, of carrying about at Christmas time a horse's skull, dressed up with ribbons, and supported on a pole by a man concealed under a large cloth, who works the jaws. The same custom was also common in one or two places of Lancashire, and in the West Riding of Yorkshire. May the custom not have something to do with the hobby-horse, of the Middle Ages, and so a remnant of the Saturnalia of the Ancients?'

THE SAGA BOOK OF THE VIKING CLUB, vol. V, pt. I, April, 1907, pp.182-183. [This contains a reprint of the extracts from Health Resort, and then proceeds:-]

Notes and Queries gives no information as to the part of Wales where the custom prevailed, but Mr. G. M. Atkinson informs us that he witnessed it in Carmarthen in 1861, and that it was then common in Wales. Mr. A. G. Moffat tells us that the custom, which the Welsh call Mary Llwyd, was common in the Swansea district till of late years, and that the Rev. J. D. Davies in his book on West Gower, vol. Ii, p.84, describes the practice as still kept up in West Gower, and that the quaint old carol called 'the twelve joys of Mary', is sung in connection with it. Mr. Davies' description of the custom is almost identical with that quoted from the *European Magazine*. Mr. Moffat does not know if the custom holds good away from the sea coast, excepting for some miles up the Swansea valley, and points out that Carmarthen is a tidal harbour. From the localities given it is possible that the custom in Wales may be due to Scandinavian influence. In any case it cannot be regarded as purely Jutish, and must have a wider significance than Mr. Whistler suggests. The horse's head fixed on a pole recalls the 'curse-pole', a horse's head fixed on a pole, set up by Egil Skallagrimsson against King Eric and Queen Gunnhilda. The turning of the horse's head landwards turned the curse on the guardian spirits of the land to force them to drive out the king and queen. The animal's heads (often horse's heads) carved on houses, looking outwards from the house, may similarly have been meant to repel evil spirits. Grimm gives several instances of the use of a horse's head in various like ways, and considered that the custom belonged equally to Celts, Teutons and Slavs, *(Footnote. – Teutònic Mythology* translated by J. S. Stallybrass, vol. II, pp.659 – 661) but he does not mention the English Hodening.

The following passages from *Keble's Margate and Ramsgate Gazette* are the result of enquiries which Mr. Sidney Shea, of Margate, was good enough to make for me in reference to the date when the custom ceased to be practised in Margate. With the exception of my letter, the following are all taken from the columns of *Local and Stray Notes*, by 'John Pharos', under which description Mr. J. P. Barrett, writes every week on local lore.

KEBLE'S MARGATE AND RAMSGATE GAZETTE, November 16th, 1907, p.2, col. 5.

Old Customs.

A friend of mine has asked me to give him any information that I may have gleaned with regard to the custom of what is termed the 'Hooden horse'. He says that as far back as 1855 the custom of carrying round a horse's head, made of wood and with moveable jaws, existed in Margate. The bearer was accompanied by various musicians, who passed round the hat. All that I know of it is that at Christmas, 1881, I saw the custom carried out at Birchington. I am under the impression that the performers came from the 'shires', that is from outside Thanet, and I have never seen it since. A young friend tells me he has seen the 'Hooden horse' at Sandwich, and thinks the party came from Deal, where I am told it is often seen. I shall be much obliged to any lover of old customs who may have seen this custom carried out, either in Margate or Thanet, if he will kindly give the date and a description of the performers and their musical instruments.

Ibid. November 23rd, 1907, p.5, col.4.

[This issue of *Keble's Gazette* contains a letter from myself describing the custom and asking for information as to the date when it was last practised in Margate].

Ibid. November 30th, 1907, p.2, col. 4.

I have to thank several friends for information concerning the old custom of the 'Hooden horse', and I hope, when time (a scarce commodity with me) permits, to trace the horses to their original stables.

Ibid. December 7th, 1907, p.2, col. 4.

Christmas Eve.

I am pleased to find that Mr. Maylam (see his letter in *Keble's Gazette* of November 23rd last) has hit upon a genuine custom formerly very common in the rural district of Thanet. From information I have received (that's good enough for the Police Court) the custom of 'Hoodening', or taking round the 'Hooden horse', on Christmas Eve was an annual one in the villages in Thanet half a century ago, and in Birchington, at least, the custom had not died out in 1906. Possibly, and I hope the wish may come true, there will be a recrudescence of the old custom next Christmas Eve, for it is a very harmless one, and I have heard of three horses' heads which still survive the ravages of time; one in Acol, another at Mutrix, and a third at Northdown. I have not yet been able to inspect either of these, but shall make further enquiries as time permits. Should the three 'Hooden horses' be brought out of their retirement, I take it that many fresh-comers into the Island would welcome them.

The 'Hooden Horse' Party.

I am indebted to Mr. Whitehead, of Margate (a native of Birchington), for a very clear description of the 'Hooden horse' party. About the year 1855, he recollects having seen as many as three parties on a Christmas Eve in Birchington. Each party came from one of the neighbouring farm-houses, where farm-servants were hired for the year and lodged on the premises. Five men formed a party, and they had no musical instruments. One man was the *groom,* who held the bridle; the second was the *horse,* he was in a stooping position, covered with a cloth, and he wore the horse's head, with a stick attached; the third was a slim youth, to represent the *jockey;* the fourth was dressed as an *old woman,* who carried a broom; and the *fifth* collected the 'oof, sometimes in a tinder box.

The Performance.

The party first sang a country song, and then knocked at the door. On opening the door the scene that presented itself was a prancing horse, opening and closing its jaws with a loud snapping noise, the groom shouting 'whoa', the jockey attempting to mount, the old lady busy sweeping and the collector looking on. If invited into the kitchen, the acting would be continued there, when, of course, the success depended much upon the ability of the various performers, who, at least, amused the little folks.

The Origin Of The Custom.

I have read several notes about the origin of the custom, but will leave that to Mr. Maylam, whom I have no doubt will be able, after his investigations, to tell us something interesting.

Mr. Earl, of Princes Street, recommends a visit to Salisbury to see the real 'Hooden horse'. Three or four years ago, when in Salisbury, I made the acquaintance of old 'Hobnob' and his giant companion, a couple of grand figures, excellent for a bonfire procession. I wish Margate possessed, as

Mr. Earl suggests, two such enormous effigies; they quite took my breath away, but alas, if the truth must be told, their appearance in the streets of Salisbury led to such riotous behaviour by the roughs that the Corporation had to prohibit the procession, and condemn the effigies to imprisonment in the Museum. They certainly are the biggest things of the kind that I have seen anywhere.

Ibid. January 11th, 1908, p.2, col.4.

Old Customs-The Hooden Horse.

I return to this subject to ask a favour. Mr. Maylam received a most interesting letter on the above subject from old residents, who wrote anonymously, and he requests that they would kindly send their names, but not for publication. I shall be glad to read Mr. Maylam's explanation of the custom of carrying round a horse's head, which seems to be of wider range than I was aware of. As one of my correspondents points out, many old customs have died out through the tendency to make them drunken orgies. In Yorkshire 40 years ago, the 'horse' died out on that account, and I learn that in Derbyshire a similar custom, known as 'snap dragon', which included a horse's head, survived even later, but the drink killed it. It was the same with 'give-ales', corrupted to 'give-alls', which were formerly carried out in church. In the 18th Century, the tenants of the 'Give-ale' lands situated at Northdown, each received a pot of beer at paying the rent, probably at the 'Six Bells', near St. John's Church. That custom has gone.

HIGHWAYS AND BYWAYS IN KENT, by Walter H. Jerrold. (Macmillan), 1907, p.116.

The ancient Christmas custom of 'hodening', here, the carrying round of the head of a dead horse, by a bell-ringing and carol singing company, was supposed to be the survival of a festival commemorating the landing of the Saxons under Hengist and Horsa, the head presumably being an example of the pun made obvious. The term hodening or hoodening is still used in some parts of the isle to denote Christmas Eve carol-singing. A Thanet Clergyman, thirty years ago, noted the old custom thus:-[Here follows in inverted commas the Old Retired Farmer's story contained in Parish & Shaw's Dictionary, which has already been sufficiently dealt with].

In *T. P's Weekly,* January 24th, 1908, there appeared an enquiry as to the custom, and the issue for February 14th, 1908, contained a reply by myself and an enquiry as to whether any similar custom is practised in Scandinavia; the *Saga Book of the Viking Club,* vol. VI, p.399 (April, 1908) also contains a note by myself in which I repeated this enquiry, but both enquiries have been without result. [8]

This concludes the references in print which I have found on our custom. I trust that this chapter will serve as a convenient record of them, but I hope the reader will not have become so saturated with the repeated allusions to the supposed festival ordained by our Saxon ancestors, as to be unable to consider any other explanation.

CHAPTER III

DISTRICTS IN KENT WHERE THE CUSTOM IS STILL PRACTISED, OR WHERE TRADITIONS OF IT REMAIN. CAUSES OF DECAY. SUGGESTION AS TO PRESERVATION.

To understand the import of this chapter frequent reference to a map of Kent will be necessary, for I propose to state the result of my research as to the districts in which the custom is now practised or has been practised in Kent within living memory. My enquiries have been as exhaustive as I could reasonably make them; anyone who has undertaken a similar search will appreciate the task. It has involved endless personal enquiries, the perusal of the files of the local newspapers (as will be seen from Chapter II) in the hope of finding more than I have found. Searching for a needle in a bundle of hay, when confident of the presence of the needle, is proverbially an unthankful business, but that is nothing to searching several bundles, when one is not sure that any needle is there at all. The information concerning Christmas contained in the local newspapers, during the period of my almost fruitless search (1840 to 1870) consists chiefly of graphic descriptions of the contents of butchers' shops, with detailed pedigrees of the oxen whose carcasses were to supply the Christmas dinners of that time.

So far as I can find, after very careful enquiry, there is now only one hooden horse party in the Isle of Thanet, that is to say, the one belonging to Hale Farm, St. Nicholas-at-Wade, and photographed at Sarre in 1905. This horse still does Sarre, Birchington and St. Nicholas every Christmas. With reference to Mr. Barrett's statement in *Keble's Gazette* (*supra* p.46) that three horses' heads had survived, one at Acol, another at Mutrix and a third at Updown, I can find no trace of these, except that the Acol horse is apparently the same as the one now at Word, of which more hereafter.

It appears that for several years no hooden horse has visited Minster, which was once the 'headest and toppingest' for it. It does not however follow that the custom is dead at Minster, for in 1868 the writer in the *Kentish Gazette* expressed surprise at seeing a hooden horse, which he thought even then was as extinct as the megatherium, but notwithstanding one came again to see how the world was jogging on – let us hope that another will come out for the same purpose at Minster in 1968.

The men on Mr. George Goodson's farm at Fenland (Felderland), Word near Sandwich, have a horse which at the proper season now goes round that district. This horse is however not a native of Word, but as Mr. Goodson explains, it was 'bred at Cleve', that is to say, it was originally made by one of the farm men who were with him at Cleve (Monkton, Thanet). Mr. Goodson went to Word at Michaelmas 1899, and about four years ago this horse came into the possession of one of his men who had gone with him from Cleve to Word, and since then it has been brought out regularly every Christmas. To survive such a transplanting shows the old custom still has vitality. The vigour of this particular horse was shown to me by accident; the presence of a hooden horse at Woodnesborough was reported to me shortly after Christmas, 1908. I knew of none in that parish and enquiries proved that it was the Word horse which had taken in Woodnesborough on its round. So far as I can ascertain, this horse when at Acol, used to visit Minster and was the last one to do so.

At Hoath, after a discontinuance of twenty years, I understand there has been a revival of the custom during the last three Christmas seasons.

A full account of the Walmer horse has been given in Chapter I, which it is unnecessary to repeat.

Lastly, there is a horse at Deal. It will be remembered that when I saw the Walmer horse at Christmas 1906, the weather prevented my going on to Deal, and in spite of many efforts I was unable to get into touch with any one connected with the Deal horse until the summer of 1909, when I made the acquaintance of Mr. Robert John Thomas Skardon, of 104, Sandown Road, Deal, who told me that he has lived at Deal all the fifty-three years of his life and had always known of the custom. When he was a lad his father used to have a hooden horse party: he carried the head, his father played the drum, his Uncle John Beaney the fiddle, and old Harry Chorner the piccolo. For many years there has been no 'Mollie', but formerly the party included a man dressed up in woman's clothes, who was known as 'Daisy'. I could find no recollection of any beginning. Skardon's uncle Beaney, who died about two years ago, aged seventy-five, had been at it all his life and his father before him. Skardon himself, it appears, about twenty years ago started a Christmas band and discontinued the horse, but notwithstanding, the hooden horse is not extinct. On Skardon discontinuing it, the custom was and is kept up by Mr. Elbridge Bowles, of 5, Fairfield Cottages, Great Mongeham; he is one of Skardon's band, but after Christmas he and one other man go round with the horse, he plays the tin whistle while the other man represents the horse. They do Deal, but finding the country districts welcome them more, of late years they have visited Finglesham, Ripple, Tilmanstone, Eastry and Betteshanger. At the time of the South African War the horse was, with great success, got up with full military equipment.

The accompanying photograph 'G' represents the Deal horse. Skardon is playing the concertina, Bowles is representing the horse. It was taken after much difficulty – a whole series of accidents arose – the performers were got together on three separate occasions before a successful picture could be obtained. The first time, owing to my well meant but inexpert assistance, the slides were mixed, so that in the case of each of three slides, one plate had two impressions and the other none; on the second attempt a thunderstorm brewed up and the resulting photographs were literally black and white, but the third attempt left nothing to be desired. I was very anxious to have a good picture of the Deal horse as the head displays a marked variance from the others. It no doubt marks a comparatively modern departure from the usual archaic type, evidently showing an attempt to be more realistic. The forehead is covered with black plush in representation of a horse's coat, the ears are made of the same material and the eyes are painted in. The animal has departed from the agricultural type, in that, between the ears, a rosette is substituted in the place of the swinging brass disc of the Thanet horse or the three bells of the Walmer horse. The covering in this case is a dark green material, a kind of box-cloth, which at one time may very well have been the lining to a billiard table or bagatelle board.

With Deal, I fear I must end the list of places where I can with certainty say the practice still survives.

The places, where the custom has only been discontinued within a comparatively recent period and where the recollection of it still remains, are so numerous and so widely distributed that one is inclined to the belief that, at no very remote period, the custom was practised throughout the whole of that part of Kent lying east of Godmersham. The only ground for setting the western boundary so far west as Godmersham is the mention of the custom by Pegge (*supra* p.27) It must be admitted that this is not a conclusive proof of the existence of the custom there, for Pegge obtained many of the words in his glossary from the Reverend John Lewis, the well-known Thanet historian, who was Vicar of Minster 'and minister of Margate in the said Island'; but on the other hand it does not of necessity follow that Pegge obtained the word from Lewis, for Lewis makes no mention of the custom in his history of Tenet – although he did not entirely neglect the folklore of the Island. It is certain that the custom has not been known or practised at Godmersham for the last eighty years; my authority being information obtained from the late Mr. Hope Theobalds who was born at Pope Street Farm, Godmersham, in 1825, and who lived in the parish the first forty years of his life.

There is no doubt that within living memory the custom was practised throughout the whole of the Isle of Thanet, including the large towns such as Ramsgate and Margate as well as the country districts. The custom has now quite died out in Ramsgate, and it is, perhaps, not strictly accurate to say it has been actually practised there within living memory, but rather that the recollection of its being practised there has not died out. My aunt, Mrs. Lacy, who is now in her ninety-seventh year and who has lived in Ramsgate since 1838, tells me the custom was never practised in that town within her recollection, but she remembers being told by a great-aunt of mine of an incident which happened to the latter in Ramsgate when a girl. One Christmas Eve (probably in the twenties of the nineteenth century) the hooden horse put its head in the door in the usual way and on her thrusting it out, the horse seized with its wooden jaws the packet of spice which she had in her hand and went off in triumph with the plunder. Mr. George Chapman, one of the Borough Magistrates at Ramsgate, who has known the town well for over sixty years, tells me, though he has never seen the hooden horse there, yet he remembers hearing of it and he always understood that the custom had been stopped in Ramsgate by the authorities, owing to a woman being so frightened that she died.

The custom would therefore appear to have died out in Ramsgate itself some time between 1807, the date of the account in the *European Magazine* (or perhaps the earlier twenties) and 1838.

As regards Margate, the custom probably lingered to a later period, and by chance I am able to fix a date at which it actually was practised at that place or at any rate the outskirts of the town. The late Mr. J. Meadows Cowper, to whom all Kent antiquarians are so such indebted, once informed me that on Boxing Day, 1855, he walked from Faversham to Margate, and on reaching Margate, being both tired and hungry – at which no one will wonder – he went into an inn (the name of which he did not remember) on the outskirts of the town for rest and refreshment and while there a party with a hooden horse visited the inn.

As stated in the last Chapter the editor of *Keble's Gazette* was good enough to insert a letter from me in his paper asking for information as to the date when the custom was last practised in Margate itself. In addition to the information contained in the extracts from *Keble's Gazette*, I received direct, two interesting communications – one from Mrs. Edward

Tomlin, of Angley Park, Cranbrook, to the effect that she remembered the hooden horse being brought to her old home, 'Updown', near Margate, in 1855, by the farm hands at Christmas time, and so far as she can remember, the last visit the hooden horse made at that place was in 1865. It appears that some words of introduction were used when the horse arrived, but what they were, my informant cannot remember; this is mentioned in view of the statement in Chapter I that no set form of words is used. The same informant states that as children, they were told that the hooden horse was supposed to be keeping up the tradition of the wooden horse celebrated in the Siege of Troy.

I also received on November 27th, 1907, the following anonymous letter:-

Sir, On reading your letter in *Keble's Gazette* I wish to say as an old inhabitant of Margate, that I remember the hoodening horse as far back as 1832. Your description of it is right, but added to the party was a man dressed as a woman – 'Molly' with a birch broom sweeping the kitchen floor where they all come inside, with several men who played the violin and fife. I do not remember what other instrument. I do not think they went about the town but mostly in country and farm houses. We lived a short distance from the town, and we children, being home for our Christmas holiday, were much amused by the performance. They were regaled afterwards with beer. After them, bellringers would come and play some old fashioned tunes such as 'Auld Lang Syne', and then lastly, some psalm singers would come and sing some beautiful hymn – the last one I remember well:

> All hail the sound of Jesu's name,
> Let Angels prostrate fall,
> Bring forth the royal diadem
> And crown him Lord of all.

As regards the country districts of Thanet the references given in the last Chapter will show that the custom prevailed everywhere until comparatively recently.

We have now finished with the practice of the custom in the Isle of Thanet and will proceed to deal with Kent outside the Island. Mrs. Edward Collard tells me that during the time her late husband lived at Dean Farm in the parish of Stourmouth (1872 to 1882), the hooden horse came every Christmas. A man dressed up in woman's clothes was one of the party, but whether known as 'Mollie' she cannot say.

There is also evidence that the hooden horse, up till about twenty years ago, visited Preston-next-Wingham, but in regard to both Stourmouth and Preston, I have not been able to ascertain whether these places possessed horses of their own or were only visited by wanderers from Thanet.

Mr. Thomas Vickers, of Evington, tells me that his mother used to speak of the hooden horse at her home at Ash-next-Sandwich [9] when she was a girl.

The remainder of Kent permits of being treated in sections. In the first place let us consider that portion of Kent which is bounded on the west by the main road from Sturry to Herne Bay, on the south by the main road from Sturry to Sarre, on the east by the Isle of Thanet and on the north by the sea. There is no question but that the custom was generally practised throughout this district down to a period of about twenty years ago; Reculver, Chislet, Upstreet, Hoath, all had the hooden horse, Rushbourne also, and Mr. Edward Fleet well recollects it at Hawe Farm, Sturry, in fact until forty or fifty years ago and Sturry village itself was visited. I was at first of the opinion that the main road from Sturry to Herne Bay was the westernmost boundary of this district, but Mr. Edward Cladish, of Blean, who himself has a faint recollection of the custom there some fifty years ago, made enquiries and was informed by an old inhabitant that boys used formerly to come round in the parish of Blean on Christmas Eve singing the following song, though they had no hooden horse:-

> Three jolly hoodening boys
> Lately come from town,
> Apples or for money
> We search the country round;
> Hats full, caps full,
> Half bushel baskets full -
> What you please to give us
> Happy we shall be.
> God bless every poor man
> Who's got an apple tree. [10]

I was afterwards able to connect this song directly with the hoodeners from information obtained from Mr. Thomas Culver of Broad Oak, a hamlet in the Parish of Sturry. He can remember the hooden horse at Broad Oak and that this was the stock song of the party, but he states that the custom has been discontinued there for quite forty years.

From Mr. Henry William Christian of Herne Common, who was born in 1839, I find that the custom was formerly practised in the parishes of Herne and Swalecliffe; he himself as a lad had many times formed one of the party, but it appears to have been discontinued in that district for years. The last time he went round with the hooden horse was when he was waggoner's mate at Chestfield, Swalecliffe, this was – that indefinite period – 'donkey's years ago'; he cannot remember the date except to this extent, that the last time he went out with the hooden horse party was the same year that he saw a policeman for the first time. Since then he has not so much as seen the horse. Among the useful purposes served by the introduction of the rural police one must therefore include that of fixing doubtful chronological points of folklore, one not anticipated by Sir Robert Peel. According to Mr. Christian the party consisted of the Hoodener, the Driver, the Jockey, Mollie, and three or four more who played the concertina, etc., and, as he says, 'bones'. He confirms the use by the hoodeners of the song furnished me by Mr. Cladish, which he repeated of his own recollection, with, however, the addition of the words given by Mr. A. Moore (*supra* p.41).

There appears to be some recollection of the custom having been observed in this district as far westward as Harbledown; Mr. James Browning, who is a woodreve at Blean, tells me that about fifty years ago for several seasons he dried hops for Mr. James Hearn at Wingate Farm[11], Wingate Hill, in the parish of Harbledown, and at Christmas time he was accustomed to go to Wingate Farm House for a Christmas Box (which in those prosperous times was of a substantial character) and to share the Christmas festivities, of which a visit from the hooden horse party formed part; though he could not remember details, the snapping jaws of the horse he had never forgotten.

We must now refer to quite another district – that lying to the south of Canterbury. There was formerly a party of hoodeners at Lower Hardres under the leadership of a man named Henry Brazier, who died about sixteen years ago at the age of eighty-six. I have seen his son John, now living at Lower Hardres, who tells me that he first went round with his father's party in the year 1857; he could not say how long before that his father had done so, but it would be for a great number of years. He could give me no information as to how or when his father had become acquainted with the custom. Henry Brazier was a famous player on the bells (not hand bells, but bells on a stand), which were struck with a stick in time and tune: these bells were always a great feature of their performances. The performers were Henry Brazier, his son John, Fairbrass, and two men named Noble. The original horse head of this party was of great antiquity; its ultimate fate was curious, as will be seen by the following tale. One afternoon, forty-nine years ago last Christmas (i.e., Christmas, 1859), they visited Lower Hardres Rectory on their round. A German gentleman and his wife were spending Christmas with the then Rector. The German lady was an invalid and had not walked for seven years. She was wheeled out in her chair on to the lawn to see the hoodeners perform. Henry Brazier, who was the horse, in the course of the customary antics made a feigned jump at her; the lady's fright was so great that she, who had not put her foot to the ground for seven years, promptly sprang out of her chair, ran indoors, and walked all right for ever afterwards. I tell the story as it was told to me, and I do not question the truthfulness of my informant, John Brazier, who saw the occurrence; but the story is not ended – the German gentleman clapped Henry Brazier on the shoulder, and said, "Well done, daddy! You have done more for my wife than all the doctors; you must sell me this horse as a remembrance." This, Henry Brazier promised to do, when the season was over. There was a party at Lower Hardres Rectory on the New Year's Eve, at which they gave a performance, and then the German gentleman bought the horse and took it with him back to Germany.

In 1860 a fresh horse was made by 'old George Noble', who appears to have been the only man in that district able to do so. This horse, some years afterwards, was bought by Squire Thomson, of Kenfield, in the parish of Petham, and another made in its place. John Brazier kept the custom up till about 1892, his father having discontinued a year or two before, but he found the absence of the bell playing a great disadvantage.

The Lower Hardres party appears to have been an important feature at the Christmas balls or parties of the country gentlemen in the district. John Brazier recollects visiting Mystole, in the parish of Chartham, in the days of old Sir John Fagg, on the occasion of a ball or party there; this happened in 1859, the same year as the incident of the German lady. They went round for a week or ten days at Christmas time and must have covered a wide district, Petham and Waltham, Upper and Lower Hardres, and Nackington, even going into Canterbury itself, where they entertained parties of soldiers in the public houses, but this was not altogether a success, the soldiers being too vigorous with their horseplay, quarrels and black eyes were the frequent result. Mr. Edward Mount Collard recollects this party visiting Sextries, in the parish of Nackington, from 1870 to 1890. Mr. Thomas Louis Collard tells me that in the early sixties (of the last century) the hooden horse used to come at Christmas to St. Lawrence Farm House, Canterbury, which was then his home, he also tells me that the Lower Hardres horse visited Winter's Farm, Nackington, until a year or two before he left that farm, which confirms the date of discontinuance, so far as concerns the company in question, as being about 1892.

The Lower Hardres horse is described to me as being 'more like a horse' than either the Thanet or Walmer horses, having a distinct neck with a white streak down the forehead and the eyes painted in; the covering sheet being of a shiny dark material. The characters in this group of performers did not include Mollie and they have no tradition or recollection of her. The proper mode of bestowing the gratuity was, as at Walmer, to put the coin in the horse's jaws; though sometimes a cap would be placed between the jaws and carried round amongst the spectators by the horse itself. They called the horse the 'hooden horse', but it also appears to have been known as the 'Christmas horse'.

I was at first of the opinion that Stelling had at one time possessed its own horse, as so many people there were acquainted with the custom, but it appears that the one which visited Stelling and Stelling Minnis was that belonging to Brazier's Lower Hardres party; my authority being Mr. Edward Mantle, who is nearly ninety years of age and has lived in Lower Hardres and Stelling all his life – he says he was well acquainted with Brazier's horse, but never knew of any other.

Mr. Thomas Vickers, of Evington, informs me that he remembers his father (Mr. Thomas Vickers, senior) telling him there used to be a hooden horse at Evington, in the parish of Elmsted, but from his own knowledge this must have been discontinued there before 1860.

There is some slight tradition of the existence of the custom at Elham. Owing to information given to me by Mr. Wanley Croft of Bridge, I went to Elham on November 2nd, 1907. I first called on Mrs. Sarah Court, who told me she would be 100 if she lived till February 24th, 1909. She was in good health and active and her mental faculties sound, but the result as to the hooden horse was blank – she had no recollection of having heard of it, but she explained that this might be accounted for by the fact that she had lived in Elham only 'a matter of sixty years or so', having been born at Acrise. I left after accepting her invitation to the celebration of her hundredth birthday [12]. I next called on a Mrs. Clayson[13] who was then eighty-eight years old. She had always lived in Elham and there had been no hooden horse there in her recollection, but she had heard her father say that when he was quite a young man they used to go round at Christmas time at Elham with a wooden horse's head. Her father's name was File, and he died some thirty years ago over eighty years of age, which of course takes us back nearly one hundred years.

There is also some doubtful trace of the custom having been practised at Chartham. I had a conversation in April, 1909, with Mr. William Jacob Hubbard, who lives at Puddledock[14], which is close to Chartham Hatch in the parish of Chartham – he was seventy-four years of age and had been there all his life, and of his own knowledge knew nothing of the custom, but he recollected a story which used to be told by his father, William Hubbard, who died about fifteen years ago, aged eighty-one, to the effect that once, at Christmas, he (that is, the father) was at Mystole, when some of the Chartham village men came with a wooden horse's head which moved its jaws, with a man underneath. His father explained that he was at Mystole in connection with his duty as one of the patrols, who were banded to protect property at the time of the stack-firing troubles in Kent. We have seen that the Lower Hardres horse certainly visited Mystole, and I think that in all probability it was the horse of that party which Hubbard saw, but my informant was certain his father said they were Chartham village men. The time of the stack-firing troubles would fix the date between 1838 and 1848.

This concludes the list of places in connection with which I have found any recollection or tradition of the custom, but in the nature of things my list cannot be exhaustive. Except in the area indicated in this Chapter, the custom seems quite unknown in Kent. It is unknown, not only in West Kent proper, but also in those parts of East Kent lying west of Godmersham. I do not think the most patient investigator would find any trace, recollection or tradition of it in the Ashford district, the Weald or Romney Marsh.

The discussion on the geographical distribution of the custom in Kent leads to a digression in the direction of dialect. Several years ago, in the course of enquiries into Kentish dialect, I was struck by the marked difference between the hooden dialect and that of the more eastern parts of East Kent, the difference being more in pronunciation and grammar than in vocabulary. The dialect, which for the sake of convenience is here termed 'Wealden', I do not suggest is restricted to the Weald of Kent, but rather that it prevails northwards as far as Faversham and eastwards until we find the East Kent dialect proper. No hard and fast boundary is put forward, but the boundary is more clearly defined than one would expect. I think that the area comprised in the present parliamentary division of St. Augustine (or perhaps better, the lathe of St. Augustine) very fairly represents the district of the East Kent dialect. Possibly a slight adjustment at the north and south ends of the western boundary of the division would make it fit in better with my theory. Quite recently I had a conversation with Mr. W. H. Hammond, who was born at Swarling in the parish of Petham, and he told me that even as a boy, when he went on a visit to Hastingleigh, he noticed how much the speech of the country folks at Hastingleigh differed from those at Petham. This difference in dialect was not in my mind when engaged in writing the present treatise until I had noted on the map of Kent the places where I had ascertained that the custom of the hooden horse is or has been practised, and I was not a little surprised to find that the custom appears to be and to have been restricted to the area over which the East Kent dialect is spoken, and that there was not trace or tradition of the custom outside that area. Curiously enough, there are other little known folk-customs which appear to have been restricted to Thanet and that part of East Kent before mentioned, concerning which on some future occasion I hope to be able to say more. Whether these facts are merely coincidences, or whether they should be attributed to some original racial or tribal difference, I do not pretend to say, I have come to no conclusions, but have recorded the facts I have noted merely for what they may be worth, I do not even know whether they clash with or confirm the theory of any writer as to the original settlement in Kent of the conquering Germanic tribes. Does the area indicated coincide with the settlement in Kent of the original Jutish tribes?

On referring to the map it will be seen that no trace or tradition of the custom has been found in the interior of St. Augustine's Division in spite of very numerous enquiries. It is possible that a search among the records of the Courts Leet, especially during the Commonwealth period would show some result, but this task – τῷ παιδί.

The cause of the decay of this custom, at any rate in late years, has I think been largely caused by agricultural depression. In the country districts the 'hooden horse' was formerly kept going by the men engaged with the horses on the farm, the horsehead, during the year, being kept in the stable. Nowadays, in many districts the arable land has been to a very great extent laid down, there are not nearly so many horses kept, and consequently, there are fewer waggoners and mates and others of that class, who formerly were particularly associated with the observance of the custom.

It seems a great pity, but probably the custom will die out in the near future, at any rate in its present natural and spontaneous form, though friendly interest can do much to keep it alive. I have only one suggestion to make, which is not original on my part, but inspired by the fate which has befallen the Salisbury giant 'Sir Christopher' and his horse 'Hob

Nob' mentioned in the last chapter – when the Corporation of Salisbury had to forbid the procession, they preserved the effigies in the city museum, and they are led out under proper control on the occasion of public processions. It seems that we might follow that example and preserve a hooden horse in the Beaney Institute at Canterbury, and when the Burgesses are allowed to unbend, as they sometimes are, and indulge in a torchlight procession, the hooden horse might very well be a feature of the show. Other towns in East Kent interested in the custom might do the same. This is my only suggestion; it is a poor substitute for natural and spontaneous observance, but it would at any rate, preserve in a way, the sense of continuity with the past, which is such an important feature in English life and customs and government.

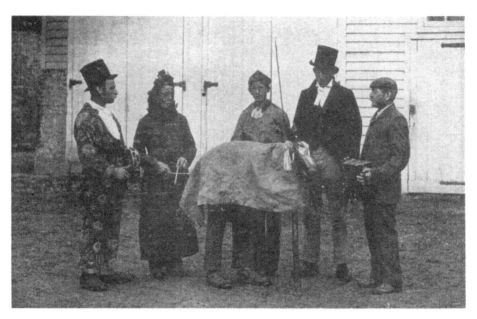

Maylam's Photo A: Hoodeners from Hale Farm, St. Nicholas-at-Wade, including musicians. Photographed at Bolingbroke Farm, Sarre, June 1905. (H.B. Collis) Full details in text.

Maylam's Photo B: Hoodeners from Hale Farm, St Nicholas-at-Wade, excluding musicians and featuring Mollie with besom broom. Photographed at Bolingbroke Farm, Sarre, June 1905. (H.B. Collis) Full details in text.

Maylam's Photo C: Hoodener who plays the horse from Hale Farm, St Nicholas-at-Wade, holding the wooden horse's head, with leather ears, head brass and face piece (trappings of a Kent farm horse dressed in state). Photographed at Bolingbroke Farm, Sarre, June 1905. (H.B. Collis) Full details in text.

Maylam's Photo D: Hoodeners from Walmer Court Farm. Photographed at Walmer, 29 March 1907. (H.B. Collis) Full details in text.

Maylam's Photo E: Walmer hooden horse rearing. Photographed at Walmer, 29 March 1907. (H.B. Collis) Full details in text.

Maylam's Photo F: Walmer hoodener holding the horse's head, with three bells (showing its place in the team of farm horses). Photographed at Walmer, 29 March 1907. (H.B. Collis)

Maylam's Photo G: The Deal Hoodeners, 1909. (H. B. Collis)

Percy Maylam, wife and child. (Maylam Family Archives)

Opposite: Percy Maylam as a young man. (Maylam Family Archives)

Left and below: Unidentified hooden horse. (Maylam Family Archives)

Above: Hooden horse party at St Nicholas-At-Wade, *c.* 1922. (Origin unknown)

Right: The Ravensbourne hooden horse. This is thought to be the horse used by Beckenham school in the 1930s. (Geoff Doel)

Photograph of hooden horse team from the article 'A Farm in Kent 100 Years Ago', by Doreen Bennett, December 1959. The photograph is undated, but two of the team are wearing Morris bells.

Hooden horse from Wingham in Maidstone Museum, 1990. (Geoff Doel)

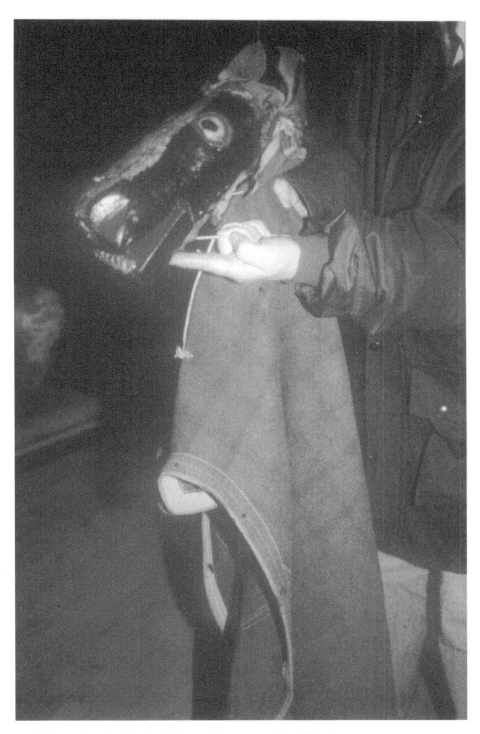

Hooden horse from Wingham in Maidstone Museum, 1990. (Geoff Doel)

Hooden horses from Wingham in Maidstone Museum, 1990. (Geoff Doel)

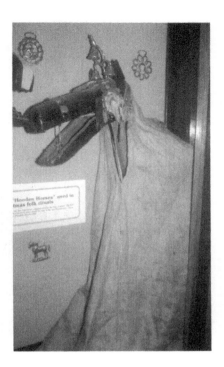

Hooden horses in Folkestone Library (now in Deal Maritime Museum), December 1996. (Geoff Doel)

Tonbridge hoodeners at Michelham Priory, 2001. (Geoff Doel)

Hooden horse convention, Gate Inn, Marshside, 2001. (Geoff Doel)

Archival photograph of Mari Lwyd Pay at Llangynwyd, South Wales.

Mari Lwyd revival at the Edmonde Arms, South Wales, *c.* 1986. (Courtesy of Mabsant)

Mari Lwyd revival at the Edmonde Arms, South Wales, c.1986. (Courtesy of Mabsant)

The Abbots Bromley horn dance, September 1893. (Alfred Parker)

The Minehead hobby hose at Quay West, 1921.

The Minehead hobby horse, 1 May 1987. (Geoff Doel)

Postcard of the Padstow hobby horse. (Fran and Geoff Doel collection)

Padstow hobby horse, 1986. (Geoff Doel)

CHAPTER IV.

Customs Of A Similar Nature To Hoodening Practised In Other Parts Of England.

There are other customs, more or less of a similar nature to hoodening, which are still practised in other parts of England and it will be useful briefly to describe them, before proceeding to discuss the origin of our Kentish custom, though to go into the matter at length is outside the scope of this present work. These customs readily allow themselves to be classified into two divisions, (1) THE HOBBY HORSE TYPE proper, being those customs in which an artificial horse or artificial horse-head forms the distinguishing feature, and (2) THE SKULL TYPE being those in which the real skull of a horse (or less frequently of some other animal) is used. It may be that there is no essential difference in principle, but one is inclined to think that these two classes have different origins, and in any event it is convenient to divide them in this way for the purposes of discussion.

THE HOBBY HORSE TYPE.

The Abbot's Bromley Hobby Horse claims the first place. It is mentioned by Dr. Plott in his *History of Staffordshire*, (p.434) who states that 'within memory, at Abbot's or Paget's Bromley, they had a sort of sport which they celebrated at Christmas, or on New Year and Twelfth Days, called the Hobbyhorse Dance, from a person who carried the image of a horse between his legs, made of thin boards, and in his hand a bow and arrow, the latter passing through a hole in the bow, and stopping on a shoulder, made a snapping noise when drawn to and fro, keeping tune with the music. With this man danced six others, carrying on their shoulders as many reindeer heads, with the arms of the chief families to whom the revenues of the town belonged'.

In *Sir Benjamin Stone's Pictures*, published by Cassell and Company (1905) there is an account of the custom as carried on at the present day, from which it appears that most of the characters wear spotted breeches of uniform pattern and carry a large pair of reindeer's horns mounted on a short pole, there are also a musician who plays on the accordion, a fool, Robin Hood and a sportsman. Robin Hood is mounted on the hobby horse, while the sportsman has the bow and arrow mentioned by Dr. Plott. This work also contains three most excellent photographs of the performers, to which I shall refer later.

The Morris Dance at Revesby in Lincolnshire. – The Folk-Lore Journal, Vol. VII, Part V, contains an article edited by T. F. Ordish giving a reprint of the words used by the dancers, from which it appears that in this case also the hobby horse finds a place among the performers, or did, so recently as the Jubilee Celebration in 1887, being represented by a man carrying between his legs the image of a horse made of thin boards. It is stated that in the early records the rider is represented as having a bow and arrow, formed in such a manner as to make a snapping noise, in the same way as the bow and arrow described in the account of the Abbot's Bromley hobby horse. The date of the performance is October 20th, but there is a reference to Christmas in the words.

The Salisbury Hob Nob. – It will be remembered that reference has already been made to this hobby horse in the extracts from *Keble's Gazette*. I am indebted to Dr. H. P. Blackmore, the Honorary Director of the Salisbury, South Wilts and Blackmore Museum at Salisbury for the following information:- Hob Nob has a wooden horse's head, the lower jaw of which is armed with sharp iron teeth and is loosely hinged on and worked by means of a leather strap. There is also a framework representing the body of a horse. When in use the whole is carried by a man on his shoulders, his head being covered by a thick cord net. He careers about after the manner of a frisky horse, and by pulling at the strap he snaps at and holds, and often tears, the clothes of any amongst the crowd of spectators. There is also in the Salisbury Museum a huge giant, 'Sir Christopher'. Both Hob Nob and the giant have figured in public processions at Salisbury for many years, on special occasions such as the Queen's Jubilee and the King's Coronation, Hob Nob, acting as the squire accompanying a feudal lord, riding before and clearing the way for the great man and the Morris Dancers who generally formed part of the procession.

The Minehead Hobby Horse. – The following description of this hobby horse has been sent to me by Mr. H. W. Kille of Avalon, Minehead, Somersetshire:- The custom of the hobby horse, as practised at Minehead, is exceedingly ancient, having been kept up from time immemorial. The structure which is termed the 'horse' bears a very crude resemblance to that animal, the wooden framework of which it is formed being covered with gaudy-coloured drapery and a profusion of ribbons. There is a hole in the middle of the back of the horse through which a man thrusts his head, which is covered with a grotesque mask and head-dress, and the framework is thus borne on the man's shoulders, his body and legs being concealed by gay houselling which reaches to the ground. In this fashion he capers about the streets, occasionally swinging round the tail, which is a long rope to which is attached a cow's tail, with considerable force, thus clearing his way. The horse is accompanied by a man with a tabor – an old-fashioned drum – and he keeps up a monotonous tum-tumming the whole time. Of course largesse is demanded of the spectators. A quaint ceremony, called 'pursing' or 'booting' was once practised on such as refused to give, but this is rarely done now. The people of Minehead are inclined rather to look askance on the hobby horse, but he still flourishes, the custom being kept up by the seamen who believe that no one can interfere with their rights so long as three rules are observed. The custom is kept up for three days at the beginning of May, and on the first day at six o'clock in the morning the party must visit a certain crossroad on the west of the town. The second rule is that on the evening of the third day at ten o'clock, they shall finish at a crossroad in the opposite direction, the third being that the custom must not be allowed to drop through, even for one year, and these rules have always been adhered to with the greatest strictness. The custom is also kept up at Padstow, but it is alleged by the Minehead sailors that the Padstow men stole the idea from them and copied their horse.

Another account of the Minehead horse will be found in *The Blackmore Country* by F. J. Snell (A. & C. Black, 1906) at p.185, where it is stated that the custom which was formerly observed at Combmartin also, is dying out.

Mrs. Story Maskelyne of Bassett Down House, Swindon, who was at Minehead this very last May Day (1909) informs me that the custom is still kept up – that on May Day Eve the town was alive with merry children dressed up as hobby horses. One huge horse perambulated the street later on, but the boys begin earlier – in small parties each with a rattle and drum. It is called a hobby or 'sailor's horse'.

The Padstow Hobby Horse (Cornwall) – *Folk-Lore* (1906) Vol. XVII, contains an article on this custom in which the horse is described as 'a formidable looking creature, with tall cap, flowing plume and tail, savage looking snappers and a ferocious mask'. So far as can be judged from the illustrations accompanying this article, the horse is built on the same lines as that of Minehead. It is taken round the streets of Padstow on the 1st of May, by a crowd of men and women, with music and the singing of May songs.

THE SKULL TYPE

Having in mind the classification mentioned at the commencement of this Chapter we will now consider those customs in which the real skull of a horse, or other animal, is used.

The Welsh custom of *Mari Llwyd* appears to be the most important. In the extracts given from Hazlitt's Edition of *Brand's Pop. Antiq.* hoodening is stated to be 'merely another form of Mari Llwyd' which previously in the same work is described as 'a horse's skull decked with ribbons which used to be carried about at Christmas time in Wales and the border counties'.

The following is a translation of a Welsh version given to Mrs. Story Maskelyne by an old Welshman from Pont Llew, Glamorganshire, circ. 1860, and which she has placed at my disposal. Judging from the conclusion it was evidently intended to be a description of the custom at the time, in spite of the reference at the commencement to the Ancient Britons. (I do not know any authority for attributing this custom to them).

PEN CEFFYL – THE HORSE'S HEAD OR MARI LLWYD

The Ancient Britons had the following curious custom at the New Year's Festival in bye gone days:- On the death of a horse, the head was severed, and buried for some months; then it was disinterred, cleaned, and shining objects were placed in the sockets in lieu of eyes. At the time of the New Year's Festival (a very ancient and important one in Wales) a chosen man enveloped in a sheet would carry the head, as though it were his own, and in this guise, with other companions, he would visit the neighbouring homesteads. On their arrival they would introduce themselves thus. Well! here we are innocent people, come for permission to sing to you this night. Then the inmates of the house would reply in verse, asking them at the same time why they wished to sing. The answer would be given in verse, which produced a competition in Englynion (Odes). When those within found themselves worsted in the conflict, they would open the doors and admit the visitors. At the sight of the horse's head they would request it to open its mouth, at which, lo and behold!, a set of horrible teeth would appear, at this sight all would feign terror and rush away shrieking. After this scene was ended and peace restored once more, tankards of home-brewed ale were brought in and money was distributed. The meeting concluded with dancing and singing till the dawn of day, when the party would break up and return to their several homes. This custom, which has survived for many centuries, is now fast dying out.

Those interested in this custom will find another account in *British Goblins* by Wirt Sykes (1880) pp.256 – 7, in which the custom is stated to prevail in various parts of Wales, notably in Lower Glamorganshire. By the same writer we are informed that the skeleton of the horse's head is decorated with favours of pink, blue and yellow, with the bottoms of two black bottles inserted in the sockets of the skeleton head for eyes, and further that the penglog (a skull, a noddle) is a similar custom in Aberconwy (Conway) in Caernarvonshire, in this case, the horse's head being an attention particularly bestowed upon prudes. According to Wirt Sykes the name Mari Llwyd (Mary Lwyd is the form he adopts) may mean Pale Mary, or Wan Mary or Hoary Mary, but the presumption is that it means in this case Blessed Mary and that the custom is of papal origin; he mentions however a tradition linking this custom with enchantment in connection with a warlike princess reported to have flourished in Gwent and Morganwg in the early ages and who is to be seen to this day mounted on her steed on a rock in Rhymney Dingle.

From information given me by Mrs. Story Maskelyne it appears that the Mari Llwyd is still taken about every year in the neighbourhood of the Mumbles, near Swansea, Glamorganshire, it was practised in Carmarthenshire at any rate in 1870; but it has not gone about in the neighbourhood of Pont Llew for the last forty years; there, it appears to have become so rowdy that the old men are ashamed to admit ever having been concerned in it [15].

Souling or Soul Caking in Cheshire – In this custom also, the real skull of a dead horse forms a prominent part, and there is such a general likeness to the Mari Llwyd, except in reference to the date of its observance, that one is inclined to believe that they are or were identical. In the extracts from *The Church Times* given in Chapter II references are made to this custom.

In Hone's *Every Day Book* (I, 1371) the subject is treated very meagrely as follows:- 'There is a custom very common in Cheshire called Old Hob; it consists of a man carrying a dead horse's head, covered with a sheet to frighten people. This frolic is usual between All Souls' Day and Christmas'.

My friend the Reverend Francis Long, who is Vicar of Weaverham in Cheshire, has made enquiries for me as to the manner in which the custom is now practised in the neighbourhood of Weaverham and Northwich, and the following short account of the custom is founded on the information obtained by him:- On November 1st and 2nd a party of men go round with a real horse's head which has been skinned, cleaned and blackened with varnish, this skull, which is decorated with plumes, bells and coloured ribbons, is fixed to a pole three or four feet long. The man who is to represent the horse fixes his head inside the horse's skull and covers his body with a rug. This imitation horse is then led round by his 'driver' to the farmhouses of the district, prancing and shaking his head and gnashing at his bit (this is done by means of a handle at the back of the skull). The other members of the party dance and sing the soul-caking song. They are dressed grotesquely and represent various characters; those usually represented are St. George, Lord Nelson, a Lady and Jack Tar. The driver of the horse then repeats a kind of speech on the merits of the horse which is called 'Dicky Tatton'. The performance closes with a chorus. The head was carried round as lately as 1907. In connection with the same custom, bands of boys and girls dressed in fantastic attire also go round at the same date from house to house singing the soul-caking song for money or whatever else they can get. In former times they expected and received a cake (hence the name soul-cake) or apples.

I have been supplied with a copy of the soul-caking song which is a variant of that appearing in Ormerod's 'Cheshire'.

The Wooset in Wiltshire – It is with some misgiving that I include a short account of this custom for it would seem to have less in common with hoodening than the other skull customs before described. It is not peculiar to Christmas or any other festival or date. According to an article by F. A. Carrington of Ogbourne St. George, apparently written in 1853 or 1854, which appeared in the *Wiltshire Archaeological Magazine*, Vol. I, p.88, the Wooset is a procession got up by way of censure to conjugal infidelity. The procession is headed by a 'rough band' beating tin kettles and old frying pans, four more carrying turnip lanterns on sticks, these are followed by a person bearing a cross of wood seven feet high, on the arms of which are placed a chemise and a horse's skull on the head of the cross, to the sides of the skull are fitted a pair of deer's horns. The lower jaw of the skull is so affixed that by pulling a string the jaws knock together with a snapping noise. The Wiltshire pronunciation of the word is 'ooset'. The writer of the article from which my information is derived saw the ceremony twice, once at Burbage in 1835, and again five years afterwards at Ogbourne St. George. I have not been able to obtain any information as to the recent observance of the custom, the reason being, it is to be hoped, that the occasions requiring the performance have become less frequent.

The last custom connected with a horse's skull to which I shall refer is that of 'Plough Monday'. In an article 'The Vikings, Their Folk-lore in Marshland' (*Viking Club Saga Book*, 1902, Vol. III, p.40), dealing with the Marshland of Lincolnshire, the Reverend R. M. Heanley says 'that for many years the "Plough Bullocks" that are due on Plough Monday have ceased to carry with them the horse's head'.

We have now left for discussion the customs in which the skull used is that of some animal other than a horse, prima facie, these have even less connection with hoodening than the horse skull type, I propose however briefly to mention them here as it may become necessary to refer to them hereafter.

The Christmas Bull – I take the 'Bull' first merely because it is the largest in size, and quote an extract from an article in the *Antiquary*, October, 1908 at p.381, *A Wiltshire Village*, by E. E. Balch:-

'Quite distinct from the mummers, though also coming on Christmas Eve, was the Christmas Bull. The head of a bull with great bottle eyes, large horns, and lolling tongue, was manipulated by a man stooping inside a body composed of a broomstick, a hide of sacking and a rope tail. The Bull knocked at the door with its horns, and, if allowed to enter, chased the young people round the house with fearsome curvets and bellowings. Even in the surrounding parishes the Christmas Bull is unknown, and I have never heard of the custom being practised in other parts of the country. The man in whose possession the Bull was until quite recently, knows that it has been in his family for over one hundred years. It was used till about ten years ago'.

The Wiltshire parish in question is Stourton. The Christmas Bull was however not confined to Wiltshire, for according to Mrs. Story Maskelyne's notes the Wassailers used to go round in West Gloucestershire at Christmas time accompanied by a man in a bull's skin, including the ears and horns with ends of bottles for eyes, and the man so dressed up used to run after the people. This was practised, at any rate, between 1830 to 1840.

This custom would apparently be the same as that described in Ditchfield's *Old English Customs* at p.28, where (after the passage relating to hoodening quoted in Chapter II) the writer states that 'at Kingscote in Gloucestershire, they have a peculiar kind of Bull Hoodening'. The expression 'Bull Hoodening' is apparently Mr. Ditchfield's own term, which, in the absence of evidence of local usage, it seems better not to adopt.

The sheep's skull appears also to be represented in places. According to Mrs. Story Maskelyne's notes, a ram's skin with something bright for eyes was taken round at Christmas in the neighbourhood of Newton and Mumbles, Glamorganshire, somewhere about 1840 to 1850. From other sources I understand that a sheep's skull is also taken round in the neighbourhood of Sheffield at Christmas, and in parts of Lancashire at Shrovetide.

This completes my list of English customs; both German and Scandinavian customs will be dealt with subsequently.

The object of this chapter has not been to propound any theory, but merely to record shortly such facts as I could obtain on customs more or less similar to the hooden horse. I shall be pleased to be informed of any such custom not referred to by me, and to receive fuller information concerning any of those which I have endeavoured to describe.

CHAPTER V.

PROXIMATE ORIGIN OF THE CUSTOM AND ITS NAME

It is useless to seek information from the hoodeners themselves as to the origin of the custom and the meaning of its name, they have no knowledge on these points and profess none, nor have they any tradition throwing any light on the question. It will be seen, however, from the extracts set out in Chapter II, that all sorts of theories have been put forward by others; for instance, in Dunkin's *History of Kent* the word 'hooden' is connected with 'hobby' and ultimately derived from 'the Gothic word 'hoppe' which signifies a horse'; in Gerald Massey's *Book of Beginnings* we are reminded of the ass's jawbone wherewith Samson slew the Philistines. I pass these over, and we come next to the theory that 'hooden' is merely a mispronunciation of 'wooden'; Mr. A. Moore, in the *Kentish Express* (*supra* p.41), says, 'a rudely cut wooden (pronounced 'wooden' or hooden by the older Kentish folk) figure of a horse's head'; Mr. Ditchfield, in *Old English Customs* (*supra* p.42) says, 'It is suggested that the wooden (pronounced 'ooden or hooden) horse's head gave the name to hoodening or goodening'[16]. It does not do to be dogmatical about anything, especially dialect pronunciation, but I do not think Mr. Moore would assert that the Kentish peasant is in the habit of pronouncing 'wooden' in the manner suggested. It is true that the horse's head is wooden, that is to say, it is made of wood; it is also true that one does hear the hooden horse called the 'wooden horse', but this is always by educated people, because, as they explain, in their opinion, that is the meaning of 'hooden'; and the statement in the *English Dialect Dictionary* (*supra* p.43) that the word 'hoodening' is locally associated with 'wooden' must not by any means be accepted as generally correct. It is perfectly clear that in the expression 'hooden horse' the pith of the meaning, the distinguishing feature, the essence of the expression, lies in the adjective 'hooden' and not in the noun 'horse', for it is the adjective alone which has given its name to the chief character, the 'hoodener', and to the custom itself, 'hoodening' and 'going a-hoodenin'. Therefore if 'hooden' merely means 'wooden', then 'hoodener' means 'woodener', and 'going a hoodening' means 'going a woodening', which tempts one to quote Euclid's triumphant quod est absurdum. Moreover, so far as Mr. Moore is concerned, in his next article on the subject, he tacitly abandoned the wooden theory in favour of the Woden or Odin derivation, as will be seen on referring to the extract on (*supra* p.41)

Another theory as to the derivation of the word has been suggested to me by persons who have been conversant with the custom all their lives, and which I mention because it has been put forward from quarters quite independent of one another. This theory is, that hooden horse means hooded horse or horse with a hood, referring to the sack under which the hoodener conceals himself. This, no doubt explains the reference to hooded horses in the extract from the *Thanet Advertiser* (*supra* p.33); but the concealing sheet is too large to be called a hood, and furthermore, this explanation does not take into consideration the paramount importance of the adjective 'hooden'.

We are now brought to the theory that the word hooden is derived from the name of the Teutonic God Woden. In this Chapter, I propose to confine the discussion chiefly to that point, that is to say, to the suggested connection between the names, in the next Chapter the matter will be discussed on broader lines. So far as I can find, this theory was first put forward in the passage from the *European Magazine* quoted in Chapter II, at least this theory is to be inferred, for after a reference to 'a Hoden or Woden horse' the passage proceeds interrogatively, 'Is the above a relic of a festival to commemorate our Saxon ancestors landing in Thanet, as the term *Woden* [17] seems to imply?'. As a matter of fact, there is not the slightest ground or justification for the expression 'Woden horse' – the term is not 'Woden' but 'hooden', if any alternative term be used at all, it is only by educated people speaking of the 'wooden' horse, because it is made of wood, as has been already explained.

In *Relics for the Curious* (*supra* p.28) after speaking of a 'Hoden or *Wooden* (*the italics are mine*) horse', the interrogative of the *European Magazine* is without further explanation changed into an affirmative, as follows:- 'this curious ceremony … is supposed to be an ancient relic of a festival, to commemorate our Saxon ancestors landing in Thanet', and the ground for this argument is varied to 'as the term *Hoden* seems to imply', which is not very intelligible, and no one will wonder that the words last quoted do not find their way into Hone's *Every Day Book*. The theory however is supported by a contributor to *The Church Times* (*supra* p.38) and Mr. Alfred Moore, in the *Kentish Express* derives not only the word 'hoodening' but also the word 'goodening' from the name 'Woden' (*supra* p.41) and expresses his opinion that the original form was 'Odinin' ' in both instances. The Reverend C. W. Whistler in his communication to *Health Resort* (*supra* p.44) says, 'hodening or hoodening is an intermediate variant of the name of Woden or Odin, which is probably Jutish, though there is a Saxon (not Anglian) tendency to pronounce an initial 'W' as an aspirate, e. g., 'William' as 'Hoolliam' ' . The meaning of the first part of the sentence is not clear. Is it suggested that 'hoodening' is an intermediate variant between 'Woden', the Low German name of the god, and 'Odin', the Norse name of the same god? If so, any authority on the point would be of interest. The alleged Saxon tendency to pronounce an initial 'W' as an aspirate does not assist us, for the simple reason that as *pronounced* by those practising the custom, there is, notwithstanding the accepted spelling, no aspirate in the word 'hoodening'.

There was a discussion in *Notes and Queries* (Ser. 9. iv, 296) as to the elision of 'w' before the 'oo' sound, in which Dr. Skeat attributed the elision (where it takes place) to Anglo-Norman influence, but so far as I am aware, there is in the East Kent dialect no elision of 'w' before the 'oo' sound.

My own impression, at first, was in favour of the Woden derivation of the word, but having before my eyes the warning of the venerable Dr. Skeat to the reckless fabricators and supporters of too obvious derivations, I investigated the matter, with the result, I must confess, that I found no sufficient evidence in proof of the theory that the word 'hooden' is derived from the name of the god Woden or Odin.

None of the supporters of this theory tell us from which of these two names it is alleged the word is derived, they appear to regard them as identical or interchangeable at will. Such of course is not the case, 'Odin' is the Norse form and 'Woden' the Low German form of the name of the same god.

The Kentish rustics who go-a-hoodening belong to the Low German branch of the Teutonic family, and it is difficult to see how a Norse name can be sufficient explanation. The arguments in favour of the Odin or Woden theory can, with reason, only be founded on the Low German variant, 'Woden'. There will be found in Grimm's *Teutonic Mythology* the forms into which the name 'Woden' has developed in the later tongues of the Low German nations, of which I will now give instances.

Grimm. *Vol I, pp. 157-158.*

> In what countries the worship of the god endured the longest, may be learnt from the names of places which are compounded with his name, because the site was sacred to him. It is very unlikely that they should be due to men bearing the same name as the god, instead of to the god himself; Wuotan, Othinn, as a man's name, does occur, but not often; and the meaning of the second half of the compounds, and their reappearance in certain regions, are altogether in favour of their being attributable to the god. From Lower Germany and Hesse, I have cited (p.151) *Wôdenesweg, Wôdenesberg, Wôdenesholt, Wôdeneshûsun,* and on the Jutish border, *Wonsild;* from the Netherlands, W*oensdrecht;* in Upper Germany such names hardly show themselves at all. In England we find: W*oodnesboro'* in Kent, near Sandwich; W*ednesbury* and W*ednesfield* in Staffordshire; *Wednesham* in Cheshire, called W*odnesfield* in Ethelwerd, p.848.

To this the translator adds a footnote as follows:-

> If numbers be an object, I fancy the English contribution might be swelled by looking up in a gazetteer the names beginning with Wans-, Wens-, Wadden-, [18] Weddin-, Wad-, Wed-, Wood-, Wam-, Wem-, Wom-.

Therefore in the name of the parish of Woodnesborough, which adjoins Ash-next-Sandwich (where, as I have shown, the custom of hoodening was formerly practised), there is, according to Grimm, admittedly preserved the name of the god Woden; and in 'Winsboro', a still common provincial alternative name for this parish [19], we have actually the form which the name Woden has taken in the tongues of the very people who call the custom hoodening. An ounce of fact is worth a pound of theory. It is clear, that in the words which are derived from the name Woden, the tendency is to preserve the initial 'W', and to elide the 'd', if not in the spelling, at any rate in the pronunciation – compare Wednesday in modern English. I therefore venture to submit, that, judging from analogy, the attempted derivation of the word hooden from the name Woden or Odin must be considered as not proved.

Something more satisfactory than mere destructive criticism, will doubtless be required of me, and therefore, having thrown stones at the windows of other people, I am now going to be so unwise as to build (what may turn out to be) a glass house of my own; the theory as to the derivation of the word 'hooden' – which seems the most likely, has the advantage of being the via media; it is not so modern and prosaic as 'wooden' or 'hooded', nor on the other hand, is it so ambitious as to go back direct to the god Odin or Woden without any resting place.

A large portion of the following remarks on the origin of the name, apply with equal force to the proximate origin of the custom. Both these points involve a consideration of the MORRIS DANCE and the older folk-games incorporated with it. One of the foremost authorities on the Morris dance is Douce, who has written a dissertation on the subject at the end of the second volume of his *Illustrations of Shakespeare and of Ancient Manners*, and the following remarks are largely based upon Douce. The Morris dance is supposed to have been introduced into England in the reign of Edward III from Spain, though Douce says it came more probably from France or even from Flanders. Strutt, in his *Sports and Pastimes of the People of England*, p.184, states that the dance was brought into England from Spain about the beginning of the sixteenth century, and that the word 'Morris' is derived from 'Morisco, which in the Spanish language signifies a Moor'. Hazlitt, in his edition of *Brand's Popular Antiquities* (I, 139) questions the accuracy of this derivation, but concedes that no better etymology has yet been proposed. Few, if any, vestiges of it can be traced prior to the reign of Henry VII, but the Churchwarden's Accounts of many parishes during the reign of Henry VIII show that the Morris dance made a considerable figure in the parish festivals. In Chamber's *Book of Days* (I, 630) it is stated that on the introduction of the Morris dance into this country it seems to have been very soon united with older pageant dance performed at certain periods in honour of Robin Hood and his outlaws. Douce (II, 439), however, referring to the suggestion that the May games of Robin Hood were nothing more than a Morris dance, in which Robin Hood, Little John, Maid Marian and Friar Tuck were the principal personages (the others being a clown or a fool, the hobby horse, the taborer and the dancers) says that this is a mistake, and explains that it is by no means clear that at any time Robin Hood and his companions were constituent characters in the Morris.

For the purposes of our discussion, it does not appear material whether the Robin Hood games annexed the Morris dance, or the Morris dance annexed the Robin Hood games, and that one of these two things happened, appears clear from the following passage from Douce (II, 444-5):-

> In the course of time these several recreations were blended together so as to become almost indistinguishable. It is however very certain that the May games of Robin Hood, accompanied with the Morris, were at first a distinct ceremony from the simple Morris ... It is probable that when the practice of archery declined, the May games of *Robin Hood* were discontinued, and that the Morris dance was transferred to the celebration of Whitsuntide, either as connected with the Whitsun ales, or as a separate amusement. In the latter instance it appears to have retained one or two of the characters in the May pageants; but no uniformity was or possibly could be observed, as the arrangement would vary in different places according to the humour or convenience of the parties.

It is to be inferred from Strutt (p.278) that Robin Hood did not originally form any part of the May games, but that, at the commencement of the sixteenth century, or earlier, it became customary to add the famous outlaw and his associates to the pageantry of the May games.

There is a painted glass window known as the Tollett window, at Betley in Staffordshire, which, according to Douce, exhibits the oldest representation of an English May game and Morris dance, and which he attributes to the reign of Edward IV. The window has twelve panes, eleven of which depict various characters, including the hobby horse, the twelfth showing the maypole. A reproduction of this window will be found in Knight's edition of *Brand's Popular Antiquities* (I, 145) and also in Gutch's *A Lytell Geste of Robin Hood*.

Perhaps the best description of the Robin Hood games cum Morris dance or Morris dance cum Robin Hood games is that contained in Strutt (pp.184-5).

> The Morris-dance was sometimes performed by itself, but was much more frequently joined to older pageants, and especially to those appropriated for the celebration of the May-games. On these occasions, the Hobby Horse, or a Dragon with Robin Hood, the Maid Marian, and other characters, supposed to have been the companions of that famous outlaw, made a part of the dance … The garments of the Morris-dancers were adorned with bells, which were not placed there merely for the sake of ornament, but were to be sounded as they danced … I do not find that the Morris-dancers were confined to any particular number. A modern writer speaks of a set of Morris-dancers who went about the country, consisting of ten men who danced, besides the maid Marian, and one who played upon the pipe afnd tabor. The hobby-horse, which seems latterly to have been almost inseparable from the Morris-dance, was a compound figure; the resemblance of the head and tail of a horse, with a light wooden frame for the body, was attached to the person who was to perform the double character, covered with trappings reaching to the ground, so as to conceal the feet of the actor and prevent its being seen that the supposed horse had none. Thus equipped, he was to prance about, imitating the curvetings and motions of a horse …

I think that any one, reading the quotations above set out, cannot fail, already to have foreseen the conjecture as to the derivation of the name and the *proximate* origin of the custom itself, which I have in mind. I suggest that the probability is that our Kentish custom under discussion is a mutilated survival of the Morris dance, not as it was on its first introduction here, but as it was, after there had become incorporated with it the older native pageants, in which Robin Hood, Maid Marian and the hobby horse formed an important part, and that 'hooden horse' and 'goinga hoodenin' ' have reference to the name of the famous outlaw Robin Hood.

Let us carefully consider the arguments. The main points in favour of this explanation are three-(1) IDENTITY OF NAME (2) THE HOBBY HORSE and (3) MOLLIE.

(1) IDENTITY OF NAME. Are we not forced to the conclusion that the 'hooden horse', the 'hoodener', and 'hoodening' take their names from Robin Hood? This identity is concealed by the hitherto generally adopted spelling 'hoden', which inaccurately represents the pronunciation, but, given a spelling based on the proper pronunciation, as explained in Chapter I, there is not only similarity between the names but identity. If, as I assume, hoodening is a relic of the Robin Hood games incorporated with the Morris dance, what could be more natural than that the custom should take its name from the chief character in these games? And indeed, the character with the hobby horse at Abbot's Bromley is still known as Robin Hood, according to the description given in *Sir Benjamin Stone's Pictures* referred to in the last Chapter.

There is another English custom which may well have derived its name also from the same source and which on that account I mention. I refer to the Hood game at Haxey, Lincolnshire, where there are every year two feasts, one on the sixth of July, called 'Haxey Midsummer', and the other on the sixth of January, called 'Haxey Hood'. The game in question takes place at the festival held on the sixth of January. The hood is a piece of sacking rolled tightly up and well corded, weighing about six pounds, this is taken to an open field and contended for by the youths assembled for that purpose. When the hood is about to be thrown up, men called the *plough bullocks* or *boggins,* dressed up in scarlet jackets, are placed among the crowd. Their persons are sacred, and if the hood falls into the hands of one of them the sport begins again. The object of the person who seizes the hood is to carry off the prize to some publichouse in the town, where he is rewarded by such liquor as he chooses to call for. The next day the plough bullocks or boggins go round the town to receive alms at each house, where they cry, 'Larguss'. They are habited similar to the Morris dancers, and are yoked to and drag a small plough. They have their farmer and a fool, called Billy Buck, dressed like a harlequin. The foregoing description is taken from an article by Mabel Peacock, in *Folklore,* (1896) Vol.VII, p.330, and the footnote to p.343 suggests that the word (i.e., hood) has an affinity with the name, Robin Hood – this is extremely probable, for the article contended for bears no resemblance to the garment called a hood, and the reference to the Morris dancers gives additional weight to the suggestion, which we can accept, without of necessity agreeing with the rest of the footnote, that Robin Hood 'is a type of spring-tide sunlight'.

The legislation which the rise of the Puritan spirit brought into force, shows to how great an extent the Robin Hood games entered into the life of the people, and how wide spread was their influence, as appears from the Acts of Parliament of Scotland, 'Queen Marie, Sext Parliament, xx of June, 1555'.

61. Anentis Robert Hude, and Abbot of Un-reason.

> Item. It is statute and ordained, that in all times cumming, na maner of person be chosen *Robert Hude,* nor *Little John, Abbot of Un-reason, Queenis* of *Maij,* nor utherwise, nouther in Burgh nor to Landwart, in onie time to cum; And gif ony Provest, Baillies, Councell and Communitie, chuse sik ane Personage as *Robert Hude, Little John, Abbotis* of *Un-reson,* or *Queenis* of *Maij,* within Burgh, the chusers of sik, sall tine their freedome for the space of five zeires, and utherwise sall be punished at the Queenis Grace will, and the acceptar of sik-like office, sall be banished foorth of the Realme; And gif ony sik persones, sik as *Robert Hude, Little John, Abbotis* of *Un-reason,* Queenis of *Maij,* beis chosen outwith Burgh, and uthers Landward Townes, the chusers sall pay to our Soveraine Ladie, ten poundes, and their persones put in waird, there to remaine during the Queenis Grace pleasure[20]; And gif onie Women or uthers about Summer trees singand, makis perturbation to the Queenis Lieges in the passage throw Burrowes and uther Landward Townes: The Women perturbatoures for skafrie of money, or utherwise, sall be taken, handled, and put upon the Cuckstules of everie Burgh or Towne.

Bishop Latimer also adds his testimony, in rather an acrimonious manner it must be confessed, as will be seen from the following extract from his sixth sermon before Edward VI:-

> I came once myselfe to a place, riding on a journey homeward from London, and I sent word overnight into the town that I would preach there in the morning, because it was a holy day, and methought it was an holidayes worke; the churche stode in my way; and I toke my horsse and my companye and went thither. I thought I should have found a great companye in the churche, and when I came there the churche dore was faste locked. I tarried there half an houre and more, and at last the keye was founde; and one of the parishe commes to me, and sayes, Syr, thys ys a busye day with us, we cannot heare you; it is ROBYN HOODES DAYE. The parishe are gone abroad to

gather for ROBYN HOODE, I pray you let them not. I was fayne there to geve place to ROBYN HOODE. I thought my rochet should have been regarded, thoughe I were not; but it woulde not serve, it was fayne to geve place to ROBYN HOODES MEN.

It is no laughying matter, my friendes, it is a wepynge matter, a heavy matter, under the pretence for gatherynge for ROBYN HOODE, a traytoure and a thefe, to put out a preacher, to have his office lesse estemed, to prefer ROBYN HOD before the mynystration of god's word; and all thys hath come of unpreachynge prelates. Thys realme hath been il provided, for that it hath had suche corrupte judgementes in it, to prefer ROBYN HODE to GODDES WORDE. Yf the bysshoppes had bene preachers, there sholde never have bene any such thynge &c.

Perhaps, after all, the good old Bishop did not in his heart object to 'Robyn Hoode's Daye', or begrudge the country people their innocent amusements, but he saw a chance of getting a home thrust at his aversion, the 'unpreachynge prelates', and it was these who moved him to such bitterness.

(2) THE HOBBY HORSE. In hoodening, the chief feature is the horse, of a distinct hobby horse type, and the association of a hobby horse with the Robin Hood games is of very ancient date. Ritson *(Robin Hood,* I, p.LVIII) gives an extract from an inventory (dated 1598) of the properties used in one of the old Robin Hood Plays, in which one finds:-

Item. i hatte for Robin Hoode, i hobihorse.

It may be said that the hooden horse differs very considerably from the popular idea of the hobby horse used in the Morris dance, as for example, that shown in Chambers' *Book of Days* (I, 631) or even from the earliest known representation of the hobby horse, that shown in the *Tollet* window before referred to; in both of these cases, the man rides or appears to ride the horse, while, in hoodening, the man himself *forms* the horse; but the less generally known forms of the hobby horse still in use, such as the Minehead Hobby Horse, the Padstow Hobby Horse, and the Salisbury Hob Nob, described in the last chapter, judging from photographs, resemble it much more closely and appear to be constructed on the same principle, in that, the man forms the horse, as in hoodening, and does not ride it, but in these cases the man is surrounded by a framework which supports the enveloping and concealing material, instead of merely having a cloth thrown over his back. In the Abbot's Bromley Hobby Horse, we find a variant of the hobby horse, which I conceive to be intermediate between the more elaborately developed hobby horse depicted in the *Book of Days*, and the more crudely shaped hooden horse; for the head of the hobby horse in the photographs of the Abbot's Bromley Morris Dance, in *Sir Benjamin Stone's Pictures*, referred to in Chapter IV, bears a strong resemblance to the head of the hooden horse. The hooden horse would appear to be either a crude, primitive, and undeveloped form of the hobby horse, or a degenerate form of what may once have been the hobby horse in all its medieval splendour; which of these two alternatives is correct, it is, owing to the total absence of record or tradition, now impossible to say. My own inclination favours the former surmise.

Though somewhat foreign to the present argument, I cannot refrain from calling attention to the similarity in mode of construction and representation existing between the hooden horse, and the mimic representations of animals described in the following passage from Strutt (p.203):-

The jugglers and the minstrels ... turned their talents towards the imitating of different animals ... On plate twenty-eight are three specimens of their performances, all taken from the fourteenth century Bodleian MS ... One of them presents to us the resemblance of a stag, and another that of a goat walking erectly on his hind feet. Neither of these fictitious animals have any forelegs: but to the first the deficiency is supplied by a staff, upon which the actor might recline at pleasure; his face is seen through an aperture on the breast ... It was also possible to heighten the whimsical appearance of this disguise by a motion communicated to the head: a trick the man might easily enough perform, by putting one of his arms into the hollow of his neck; and probably the neck was made pliable for that purpose.

Although the horse is not included among the animals in question, a reference to the plate will show that they are constructed and mimicked somewhat in the same way as in the case of the hooden horse, more especially the Walmer horse, which has a peephole through the sack cloth at the junction of the head with the upright staff, as will be seen from photograph 'E'.

(3) MOLLIE. The presence of Mollie is another strong link in the chain of evidence connecting the hooden horse with Robin Hood. Maid Marian, the mistress [21] of the outlaw, was a well known character in the Robin Hood group. Originally the part of Maid Marian was acted by a woman, probably of beauty, and no doubt suitably attired, but according to Douce (II, 457), after the Morris degenerated into a piece of coarse buffoonery, Maid Marian was personated by a clown, and the once elegant Queen of the May obtained the name of 'Malkin'. This degeneration must have taken place at a comparatively early period, for in Cobbe's *Prophecies, his Signes & Tokens, his Madrigalls, Questions & Answers* of the year 1614 (quoted in *Hone's Year Book*, 836) the following verses occur:-

It was my hap of late, by chance,
To meet a country Morris dance
When, cheefest of them all, the foole
Plaied with a ladle –
When every younger shak't his bells –
And fine Maid Marian, with her smoile
Shew'd how a rascall plaid the roile ;
But, when the hobby-horse did wihy,
Then all the wenches gave a tihy.

Shakespeare too, in Henry IV, pt. I, Act iii. Sc. 3, refers to the then degenerated form of Maid Marian. I think, therefore, that one is justified in identifying the hoodener's Mollie (a variant of Mary or Marian) with Maid Marian in the Robin Hood group.

The following contribution to *Notes & Queries* is of interest as showing that my suggested connection of Mollie with the Morris dance is not without support:-

Notes & Queries. Mar. 4, 1882 (6 Ser., v, 176).

On Plough Monday troops or 'sets' from neighbour-villages annually visited the town. In the costume, which formed no small part of the rivalry of the sets, the most noticeable points were brown or black velveteen coats, covered with bows and streamers of bright ribbons; tall hats banded from brim to crown with ribbon and adorned with a plume of feathers. Each troop was accompanied by a 'Moll', a swain dressed as a woman, generally in white muslin or extravagantly in the latest fashion. Dances were formed at intervals through the main streets, and largess solicited. An important feature with some troops was a wooden plough drawn by four or six of the company; this formed the centre of a 'round dance'. The Madingley set was famous (about 1848) for their get-up and that of their 'Moll'. There was always a marked courtesy shown to the 'Moll' which may have had an origin in some earlier form of Morris dancing; of this I should be glad to learn something. I believe the custom is still observed though possibly with 'maimed rites'. W. R. Chelsea.

In addition to the three main arguments which have been just discussed, there are in hoodening a few details, in which possibly the influence of the Morris dance may be traced, but these are subsidiary points, and the resemblance may be merely a coincidence. I shall therefore not labour these points, but they should be mentioned.

The sheep bells formerly used at Walmer, may be a survival of the bells attached to the dress of the Morris dancers mentioned in the quotation from Strutt; and the fact that the Thanet hoodeners occasionally blacken their faces, should be remembered in connection with the statement that the Morris dancers usually blackened their faces with soot, that they might the better pass for Moors. (Douce II, 434.) The musicians accompanying the hoodeners correspond to the players on the tabor, etc., of the Morris dancers, and the fantastic dress worn by the tambourine player in the photograph of the Thanet Hoodeners, is in keeping with what is known of the Morris dance (there were three characters in the play performed by the Revesby Morris dancers, known as Blue Breeches, Pepper Breeches and Ginger Breeches, whose names speak for themselves); but as regards costume, it must not be forgotten that the earliest tradition speaks of smock frocks being worn by the hoodeners. It may be that the strong dark material, before-mentioned, of which the covering of the hoodener was made, in the case of the Lower Hardres horse, is of an older type than the coarse sacking used by the Thanet and Walmer hoodeners, for a footnote to Ritson (I, CVI) states that 'Black buckram appears to have been much used for the dresses of the ancient mummers'.

It will be remembered that the gratuity in the case of the Walmer hooden horse is accustomed to be placed in the jaws of the horse, and in the case of the Lower Hardres horse, the money was also placed there, or in a cap inserted in the horse's jaws for that purpose; in view of this, it is curious to note that Douce (II, 468) tells us that a ladle was suspended to the mouth of the Morris dance hobby horse for the purpose of gathering money from spectators [22], though in later times the fool appears to have performed this office.

It is now time to consider certain points which at first sight may appear to tell against the Robin Hood theory, but which on examination present no real difficulty.

It may, for instance, be said that the hooden horse custom is hoodening at Christmas time, while we are accustomed to regard the Morris dance and Robin Hood games as being performed especially at the summer festivals – at May Day and Whitsuntide, but they cannot have been restricted to the summer, for we find the Abbot's Bromley Morris dancers with their hobby horse celebrating 'at Christmas or on New Year and Twelfth Days'.

The date of the celebration of the Revesby Morris dance is in October, but we find the following among the words used:-

'Still we are all brave jovial boys
And take delight in Christmas Toys'.

and a reference to 'this good time of Christmas'.

Strutt (pp. 183-184) was of the opinion that the Morris dance originated from the fool's dance, which he surmised, formed a part of the pageant belonging to the festival of fools – a religious mummery usually held at Christmas time.

Douce (II, 440) tells us:-

> that other festivals and ceremonies had their Morris; as Holy Thursday; the Whitsun-ales, the bride-ales, or weddings; and a sort of play or pageant called the lord of misrule.

The last mentioned clearly referring to Christmas time.

In Chambers' *Book of Days* (I, 633) it is stated that:-

> A tract of the time of Charles I entitled *Mythomistes,* speaks of 'the best taught country Morris-dancer, with all his bells and napkins', as being sometimes employed at Christmas; so that the performance appears not to have been absolutely limited to any period of the year, though it seems to have been considered as most appropriate to Whitsuntide and the month of May.

It would appear therefore that the date of celebration presents no obstacle to the acceptance of our theory.

It must have occurred to the reader, that I have quoted no authority, showing that the Robin Hood games or the Morris dance were practised in East Kent, even in the height of their fame, but I am unable to do so. It is true, there is the well known instance of the pageant arranged by King Henry VIII for the benefit of his Queen (Katherine of Aragon) at Shooter's Hill on May Day in an early year of his reign. This is not very satisfactory – Shooter's Hill is not East Kent by a long way. On this point, however, the following curious reference to the Morris dance, is perhaps worth mentioning, in view of the locality it concerns – Arch. Cant., vol. Xxv at page 107 quotes from a letter dated January 8th, 1640-1, from Richard Culmer [23] to Sir Edward Dering as follows:-

> I have had very ungracious dealeing from the Lambeth Patriarch, by whom I have bene deprived of my ministry [Goodneston], and all the profitts of my Liveing three yeares and seaven monthes, haveing my selfe, my wife, and seven children to provide for; such is the Prelates tyranny for not consenting to Morris daunceing uppon the Lords day.

It is therefore clear, that Culmer, a man of Kent, who was born in Thanet and had been to school at Canterbury, and who had been deprived of the living of Goodnestone, was evidently acquainted with the Morris dance, though of course the above may merely be the protest of a Puritan divine against an elaborate ritual, which he impolitely compares to a Morris dance.

It may be useful, shortly to summarise, the results I have sought to establish in this chapter:-

(1) That 'the hooden horse' and the custom 'hoodening' have been named after the famous outlaw Robin Hood.

(2) That in the hooden horse custom, we have a survival of the old pageants of Robin Hood, Maid Marian and the Outlaws of the Band, which were afterwards incorporated in the Morris dance.

(3) And that, perhaps, in our custom we have these old pageants, preserved in their crudest and most primitive form, and comparatively but little affected by the influence of the Morris dance.

If the first two points are established, we have ridden our hooden horse a long way back into the past, though possibly not to the desired goal – 'his original stables' – and it is evident that any further research into the origin of the custom becomes involved in the origin of the Robin Hood games and of the hobby horse.

After the preceding part of this chapter was written, two very important matters came before my notice, which can better be dealt with in the form of a continuation than by incorporating them in my previous arguments.

The first matter is a piece of strong evidence in support of the theory connecting hoodening with Robin Hood and the Morris dance.

Wishing to ascertain if there were any tradition of the hooden horse in the Sandwich district, I made enquiries on that point of Mr. G. C. Solley of Richborough, Ash-next-Sandwich, and the information which was the result of my enquiry, I will set out in Mr. Solley's own words, as follows:-

> My father, George Solley, was born at Richborough Castle Farm on St. Thomas's Day, in 1814; he lived there nearly all his life and died at Sandwich in 1899. He has told me that when he was very young, (about ten years old he thought), a party of hoodeners from Ash used to come round on the *day* before Christmas Day. Some of the party were dressed up as fools and there was with them a Maid Marian (this was his own term and he explained it as being a man dressed up in woman's clothes). One of the party had a kind of black rug thrown over him, and carried a horse's head, which kept nodding about. He remembered seeing the hoodeners knocking one another about with sticks and bladders on the green at the back of our house. I myself was born at Richborough and I recollect that about 1872, for some years, two old men used to come on Christmas Eve singing songs. We always called them the 'hoodeners' though they had no hooden horse.

The importance of this communication is apparent, as it connects the Mollie of the present day Thanet hoodeners, directly by name, with Maid Marian and as a consequence with Robin Hood, with whose name that of Maid Marian is inseparably joined. Possibly, too, the reference to some of the party being dressed as fools and knocking one another about with bladders, takes us back to the 'dance of fools' from which Strutt suggests that the Morris dance originated.

Mr. G. C. Solley gave me this information without being aware of my theory and without any reference having been made to Robin Hood or Maid Marian.

The second matter which has come to my knowledge since this chapter was written, has reference to Robin Hood, and also to the Woden theory, and it would be out of keeping with the character of a patient and impartial investigator if the matter were not gone into, for, although it gives the support of the German folklorist Kuhn to the connection between hoodening and Robin Hood, which I had also independently arrived at, yet at the same time, it approves of the Woden theory.

My attention was in the first place drawn to the following passage from Grimm's *Teutonic Mythology* (Vol. II, p.504):-

> Wouter, Wolter is nothing but the human proper name Walter bestowed on a home-sprite. It is quite of a piece with the familiar intercourse between these spirits and mankind, that, beside the usual appellatives, certain proper names should be given to them, the diminutives of Henry, Joachim, Walter. Not otherwise do I understand the *Robin* and *Nissen* in the wonted names for the English and Danish goblins *Robin goodfellow* and *Nissen god dreng*. Robin is a French-English form of the name Robert, OHG. Hruodperaht. MHG. Ruotperht, our Ruprecht, Rupert, Ruppert; and *Robin fellow* is the same home-sprite whom we in Germany call *knecht Ruprecht*, and exhibit to children at Christmas [24], but who in the comedies of the 16-17th centuries becomes a mere *Rüpel* or *Rüppel*, i.e. a merry fool in general. In England, Robin Goodfellow seems to get mixed up with Robin Hood the archer, as Hood himself reminds us of Hôdeken [a home-sprite at Hildesheim, so called from the felt hat he wore]; and I think this derivation from a being of the goblin kind, and universally known to the people, is preferable to the attempted historical ones from Rubertus a Saxon mass-priest, or the English Robertus knight, one of the slayers of Thomas Becket.

and *ibid*. Vol. IV, p.1432:-

> In Holstein they called knecht Ruprecht *Roppert* with whom and with Wôden Kuhn compares *Robin Hood,* Hpt's Ztschr. 5, 482-3.

The last passage in particular seemed worth further enquiry, therefore, at the British Museum, I referred to Haupt's *Zeitschrift für Deutsches Alterthum*, Vol. 5 (1845), which contains a long article on Woden by A. Kuhn, who was a well known German folklorist of the early Grimm school. A perusal of the extracts from Kuhn's article will show that he arrived at two conclusions: (1) That the name 'hooden' is to be derived from Woden, and (2) That the custom of hoodening is connected with Robin Hood, or as Kuhn puts it, that the name 'Hood' is a *corruption* of the word 'hoodening'. I reserve discussion on these points for the next Chapter, which contains full extracts from Kuhn's article, together with extracts from other German writers.

CHAPTER VI.

ULTIMATE ORIGIN. GERMAN CUSTOMS OF A SIMILAR KIND, SCHIMMELREITEN, ETC.

Although the theory set out in the last chapter may explain the origin of the name 'hooden horse', and the *proximate* origin of the custom, yet there remains the question – can the origin be traced still further back?

The custom of carrying round at Christmas and other times the head, real or artificial, of a horse, or less frequently, of some other animal, which shortly may be called the horse-head custom, is practised over such a wide area and in so many countries, not all affected by the Robin Hood cult, that one is tempted to believe, that the old pageants of Robin Hood must themselves have been attached to yet older pageants of the horse-head or hobby horse type.

The ultimate origin of the hooden horse unquestionably affords a vast field for speculative demonstration to those, who are endowed with ample imagination and the inclination to regard any faint analogy as actual proof of identity; this is more especially the case if, in addition to possessing these mental qualities (and perhaps therefore), they belong to the great 'Wenn' [25] School of Folklorists. Anything can be proved, or disproved, provided one can at will substitute non-existing circumstances for those actually existing. Under these conditions, Gerald Massey, in the extract from the Book of the Beginnings (*supra* p.35), has shown our custom to be a variant of the solar myth, and connected it with the story of Samson slaying the Philistines; under similar conditions it has been successfully proved that neither Gladstone nor W. G. Grace ever had any actual existence, they also being merely variants of the solar myth. Any one with a gift in this direction can doubtless connect our custom with the European Sky-god or with totemism, and introduce it as a fresh factor into the geometrical problems, which prove that the Australian blackmen may or may not marry their great-grandmothers.

I myself have no inclination to undertake the task of pyramid building with a single truss of straw and one wheelbarrow load of clay, and therefore I propose to restrict my enquiry to this – can we reasonably connect the ultimate origin of our custom with the ancient worship of our pagan Teutonic ancestors, and in particular with the worship of Woden? Even with this restriction we find ourselves skating on the very thin ice of surmise. The discussion in the last chapter on this point was chiefly confined to the origin of the name, and the question generally remains for consideration.

By way of preface to the following discussion, and as a warning of the length to which it is possible to go in an attempt to show connection between modern folk-practices of today and the religious observances of our Teutonic ancestors, and showing the scrutiny to which such attempts should be subjected, I will refer to a contribution in *Folklore*, 1896, vol.VII, p.298. The writer of the passage in question had in 1893, at Island Road Farm, otherwise Westbere Court Farm, in the parish of Westbere, Kent, seen the dead body of a sheep in a tree, and this circumstance induced a comparison with the Grove of Upsala, 'there hang the bodies of dogs and men alike', and the article is headed 'a survival of Odin worship in Kent'. It is true, that it is a common practice in Kent, and doubtless in other counties, to put up in a tree the carcasses of sheep which have died a natural death, and are therefore unfit for human consumption, but, as a matter of fact, the object of doing so is purely utilitarian and not superstitious; such carcasses are saved for the specific purpose of providing food for the farm dogs, and are put up in a tree to keep them out of the way of the dogs, except when savoury pieces are cut off for them at proper intervals. There was one tree in an orchard at my old home (Pivington in the parish of Pluckley), which I, as a child, knew as 'the dogs' pantry', because that tree in particular served this purpose. If not saved with an object, the carcasses would be buried out of the way and not used to ornament trees. It is, of course, not pretended that the alleged connection between the hooden horse and Woden can be dismissed in such a summary manner.

In the last Chapter it was pointed out that the interrogative of the *European Magazine*, 'is the above a relic of a festival to commemorate our Saxon ancestors landing in Thanet?' had, in the subsequent versions, founded on that of the *European Magazine*, been transposed into the affirmative, without further explanation; but, for detailed arguments in favour of the theory that the hooden horse is a relic of the worship of Woden, we must go to the early German folklore writers, for this theory was 'made in Germany', years before the Merchandise Marks Act, 1887, or rather the arguments in favour of this theory were formulated there.

To this day, in various parts of Germany there are customs, varying in form, which bear a marked resemblance to our Kentish hooden horse. Any custom which the Kentish countryman possesses and practises in common with his continental cousins must naturally have had a very ancient beginning, *if* a common pre-Christian origin be proved. It is therefore essential that these German customs should be described and considered. I propose now to give translations of the passages from German writers which I have found bearing on the subject, and afterwards to discuss the effect and weight of the arguments.

MÄRKISCHE FORSCHUNGEN herausgegeben von dem Vereine für Geschichte der Mark Brandenburg 1ster Band, Berlin 1841. ('Über das Verhältniss Märkischer Sagen und Gebräuche zur Altdeutschen Mythologie', von Adalbert Kuhn).

[*Translation*]

(p. 117) We find in the Mark, no exact and sure indication of the male deities of the higher rank, for only scanty traces have been retained of the worship of them, as Grimm's collection has already shown. At the same time, solitary references and customs show that recollection of them has not yet quite died out, and it is of Woden and Thor, that I believe I have found some remembrance.

As regards Woden, I include a custom which to the present day prevails at Christmas in the County of Ruppin. Lads and maidens assemble of an evening, in the week next before Christmas. One of the lads imitates the figure of a Rider on a White Horse (Schimmel), a sieve or a similar utensil is fastened on to his breast in front, and another on to his back, over which is hung a white linen cloth; another, also clad in white, and decorated with ribbons, who carries a big bag, is called the Christmann or the Christ-puppe. Several of the others dress themselves up as old women and blacken their faces. These are called die Feien (the Fays). When all these preparations are done, the procession starts, and goes with music from house to house, accompanied by all those assembled, and children join on with shouts of glee. On entering the living room, a chair is set before the Rider over which he has to jump. This being done, the Christ-puppe enters with the accompanying crowd, the Fays only not being allowed to enter. The girls then sing a song, the tune of which is always the same, but the words of which vary, though at places a set form of words may be used. The Rider now chooses from the band of maidens one with whom he dances to music in the following manner: standing opposite one another they both make all sorts of twists and turns, in accordance with their fancy. While this is in progress, the Christ-puppe goes around among the children and enquires whether they can say their prayers. If they repeat a verse from the Bible or prayerbook, they are rewarded with a peppercake from the big bag, but if they cannot they are beaten with the ash bag. Thereupon, the Rider as well as the Christ-puppe dance with some of the crowd and then depart, this dance closing the chief part of the ceremony. During the whole of the proceedings before described, the Fays have not ceased in their attempts to force their way in, but each time have been driven back with jokes and ridicule of all sorts, at last, after the Rider and the Christ-puppe have left the room, they press in, and jump around in a wild and boisterous manner, beating the children, it being their chief endeavour to put everyone in a fright. These proceedings are repeated at every house, one or more being visited in an evening, according to the greater or less number of farm houses in the village.

Unless we are mistaken, recollections of ancient heathendom are to be found in this procession, as in almost all of the few, which have been preserved to us at the present day. This ancient heathendom has lost the day and Christianity has won the victory over it; the Christmann goes freely into the houses of men, but the old goddesses of fate, the Fays, have no longer entrance therein, and they dare approach only when the Christkind has withdrawn. They scare and frighten the children by their wild and boisterous manner, but the Christmann praises and rewards the good, and punishes only the naughty, who cannot say their prayers. So also in other places appear the rough bearded Knecht Ruprecht and Knecht Niclas, the frighteners of children (compare Grimm's *Teutonic Mythology*, p.294), they are likewise ancient heathen forms and primitive house-sprites, but who have obtained a more christian shape, and in a certain degree serve the Christmann. For Christianity, which can make even the water sprites blessed, as the touching Swedish story tells us (G. *Teut. Myth.*, p.279), has also taken the two house-sprites into her bosom, and if she could not take from them their rugged exterior, she has diverted them to her own mild purposes - repentance and amendment. But blind destiny, that cruel governing fate, she dared not permit to exist near her, and on that account, we here see the Fays shut out, whose race we with Grimm (G. *Teut. Myth.*, p.232) pronounce to be from fatum or rather from a new formed fem. fata. Besides the Fays, there appears with the Christmann yet another figure, which at all events is of great importance, for really the whole proceedings revolve around it, namely the Schimmelreiter, in whom, unless everything receives us, we recognise Woden. He is frequently, in Lower Germany, in isolated passages from traditions, represented as a Rider; in Mecklenburg, in harvest time, they leave a sheaf of corn standing 'to Woden for his horse' (G. *Teut. Myth.*, p.104), and northern tradition, according to Grimm's confident conjecture, points out this horse as a white horse (G. *Teut. Myth.*, p.532), and so also, the white horse is almost always attributed to the other leaders of the Raging Host (G. *Teut. Myth.*, p.519-34). I find a further support for my conjecture in the fact that the Fays appear in this procession, for the goddesses of Fate are chiefly connected with Woden, with Odin, the all-knowing All-Father; lastly, the date of the festival seems to me to be of importance, for Woden and Frau Holla stand in close connection, indeed they are often almost identical, allowing for the difference between male and female. Ought not therefore, the twelve nights [of Yuletide] to be the festival of the god ? as they are the festival of the goddess. Hackelbernd, an especial personification of the Wild Huntsman, who is particularly known in the Altmark, goes through the country during the twelve nights only, and Hackelbernd and Woden are identical, according to all that Grimm has said concerning them both (G. *Teut. Myth.*, p.519). I believe therefore, that with some degree of probability, we may recognise Woden in the Rider on the White Horse, who here takes part in our procession, for the manner in which he makes his appearance, shows that the intention is to draw a contrast between Christianity and heathendom, and to represent the conquest of heathendom, and no one is adapted to this purpose, better than he, who was the highest of the ancient gods, and who now must dance and jump about – the laughing stock of the crowd, and this in the presence of Him, to whom the children must say their prayers.

MÄRKISCHE SAGEN UND MÄRCHEN nebst einem Anhange von Gebräuchen und Aberglauben (Adalbert Kuhn, Berlin, 1843).

[Translation]

Preface, p.v. The chief result of these researches is the proof that nearly all the mythological recollections of our country people are of Teutonic origin. The writer has already discussed this point in detail in the first volume of the Märkische Forschungen [in the treatise on the relation of the Traditions and Customs of the Mark with old *Teutonic Mythology*] and even if he now rejects as no longer tenable, some of the opinions there put forward, yet he still, as then, defends the gist of these opinions. It appears indeed, now and then, as if our people have preserved some things of Slavonic origin, but these are so small, that, in comparison with the Teutonic, they are not worth consideration; at any rate, if they should be present in a greater degree, they can only be of an incidental nature, for they are so allied with the Teutonic that a distinction is not at all possible. Therefore, while using as a foundation, the assertions contained in the treatise before cited, we propose shortly to emphasise those points which appear to be worthy of particular mention.

Whether the Rider on a White Horse, who appears on several occasions (see Christmas, Shrovetide, and Wedding Customs) accompanied by the Fays (the old goddesses of Fate) is Woden, as I assumed in the above treatise, I now leave undecided, for this figure has neither a precise name, nor are there existing, any special customs whatever, which point to the acceptance of this theory. The only ground for the conjecture lies in the appearance of the Fays with him, and somewhat in the form of the Rider, in a broad-brimmed hat and large cloak, as he appears in the Altmark in particular; perhaps also, in the peculiar punishment for those who withdraw from the wedding company in Prignitz (Customs, p.362), for in Christian times it was no longer permitted for anyone to represent the pagan god, and only punishment could be entailed by doing so.

Ibid. Customs and Superstitions, p.307.

Shrovetide. In some districts [of the Mittelmark] a Rider on a White Horse is represented in the following manner: a sieve is fastened on to one of the lads in front and another on to his back, which is covered by a white cloth, and a horse's head is fixed in front. The Rider then prances about in all sorts of funny ways to the amusement of the company. In other places, an ox is made up in a similar way, and is then slaughtered; a big pot is fastened to the forehead of the person representing the ox, on to which the blow is directed, general mirth of course follows a successful stroke.

Ibid. Christmas and the New Year p. 346.

[Here follows an account of the appearance of the Schimmelreiter in Ruppin as before described by the same writer, (*supra* p.94)

Ibid. p. 361.

The procession of the Rider on a White Horse already described, is also found at weddings, namely in the Altmark at Wassensdorf, Beetzendorf, Wadekath and other places. He appears on the first day of the wedding, which here would be Thursday. The Rider wears a cloak made from a red petticoat, and a large broad-brimmed hat which the country people call 'Puust de Lamp uut' (put the lamp out). The Rider jumps about in a marvellous manner; one of the company plays the part of the smith and sees whether the hoofs are in proper condition, which the restive animal of course will not allow – and much more of the same sort of thing. At Prignitz, in the neighbourhood of Lenzen, those who withdraw from the wedding company to rest a while, are punished in the following manner: search is made for them as soon as they are missed, and then two of the company buckle a saddle on to a tree trunk kept ready for the purpose, this the sleepy one is forced to mount, and so riding is brought back to the assembled guests. In the county of Ruppin, the Fays (who, as already stated, are generally men dressed up) appear as the wedding procession is approaching the church, and endeavour to upset the festive procession by all sorts of pranks, and to turn their seriousness into laughter.

ZEITSCHRIFT FÜR DEUTSCHES ALTERTHUM herausgegeben von Moriz Haupt. Leipzig 184-5. fünfter Band. ('Wodan', von A. Kuhn).

[Translation]

(p.472). In the first volume of the *Märkische Forschungen* (pp.117 – 120) I have already expressed a conjecture that the form of a Rider on a White Horse, which appears on various occasions, for instance among the Christmas customs, is intended to represent Woden. Since then, in other districts of Germany and also among English customs, there have been discovered processions, which raise this conjecture almost to a certainty, and at the same time make significant, a number of other points connected with this custom; so that a more exact consideration and examination of it will not be without profit.

In the first place, as regards the description of the way in which the Rider is made up. Among us in the Mark, as well as in the rest of North Germany as far as the hilly districts, it is usual for this purpose to tie sieves before the breast of a young lad and on to his back; to the sieve in front, a short rod is fastened, on the end of which is fixed a horse's head, always kept ready for that purpose; white sheets are then spread over the sieves, so that the whole represents a rider on a white horse-in a crude manner it is true, but still recognisable enough. At Drömling in the Altmark, the rider is always furnished with a broad brimmed hat and a large mantle made of a red petticoat. In several places there is another feature besides; to the lower jaw of the horse's head a string is fastened in such a way, that the rider is able, by pulling and loosening the string to make a snapping noise. The figure formed in this manner is generally, for short, called the 'Schimmel', and usually appears in connection with other figures – almost everywhere of a similar character. These are, first the so- called bear – a young lad completely concealed in pea haulm, who is generally led on an iron chain; then the smith, who has to see whether the hoofs of the horse are in proper order; lastly, in some places in the Mark, there are the Fays also, young lads with blackened faces, and clad in women's clothes. At places there are other figures in addition, according to the time at which the custom takes place. At Christmas, for instance, when the custom is most frequently practised, knecht Ruprecht, as well as der heilige Christ, almost always make an appearance with the Rider. In some places however, especially in the neighbourhood of Halle, the Rider himself is called Ruprecht. So, in the Isle of Usedom, the custom as a whole, is designated, the going round of Ruprecht who makes the children say their prayers. Here three figures appear, one with a big stick and an ash bag, and concealed in pea haulm, as is the case with the bear which is taken round in other places; the second carries a so-called Klapperbock[26], a staff over which a goat's skin is stretched and to which a wooden head is fastened, which has an arrangement for making a snapping noise similar to that of the horse's head before described; with the Klapperbock he pushes about the children who cannot say their prayers; lastly, the third appears as Rider on a White Horse.

I have already stated in the *Märkische Forschungen*, and also in my *Märkische Sagen und Märchen* (pp. 308, 345, 361) that this Rider appears at Christmas-time as well as at Shrovetide and at weddings; to which I will add, in connection with the conjecture I expressed in a former passage, that at Warthe, near Templin, in the Übermark, three such Fays, but without the Rider, formerly appeared at weddings, with whom the bride was obliged to dance. Besides these two fixed periods of the year the Rider also appears at Whitsuntide. In the district of Sangerhausen especially, on the second day of Whitsuntide in many villages, a riding contest for a hat is arranged. The first at the winning post is King, and receives as prize a hat, which is stuck up on a pole, a silk handkerchief or the like. This custom is followed by a dance, at which the Schimmel usually appears; he also shows himself at Bockenem, in Hildesheim, on the occasion of the shooting festival, which is held every year in the summer, but on no fixed day. Just such another Rider on a White Horse appears nowadays in England, of which the name and the customs connected therewith throw more light on the whole matter. I borrow the report treating of this chiefly from a periodical, the *Mirror*, which has appeared since 1826, and which interests itself particularly in the description of English folk-customs … [Here follow descriptions of the Padstow Hobby Horse, *Mirror*, vol. I., and of the Abbot's Bromley Hobby Horse, *ibid*. vol. XIX, p.228.] … The third account corresponds the most exactly [Here follows the quotation from the *Mirror* relating to the hooden horse (*supra* p.29) beginning with the words 'at Ramsgate, Kent', and ending with the words 'some religious ceremony practised in the early ages by our Saxon Ancestors'.] … These descriptions show plainly that the customs they describe are completely identical with our custom, only the arrow and boy mentioned in the second description are wanting in ours. The correspondence, even in detail, proves conclusively that the custom is primeval [27], as the author of the third description conjectures. There are not wanting proofs of the appearance of the English custom in the sixteenth century, for in vol. XXVI, p.423, a writer of this period is mentioned, who, speaking of christmas mummery, says, … [Here follows a long passage describing the lord of misrule.] … These customs, which were a vexation to the Church, as is shown by the description, could not then have first come into existence, for they were there before the Reformation, and that they survived this, shows how deeply they were rooted in the hearts of the people. The whole character of these customs shows their pagan origin, and thus we may without hesitation regard the name *hooden*, which the Rider bears, as *Woden,* and indeed the expression *wooden horse* itself leads the way to such conclusion [28]. The ancient *ô* has changed into *oo*, and the change of the *w* into *h* before the *u* sound is so natural in English that we ought to look for numerous examples, which perhaps are to be found in the dialects [29]. Other languages show it plainly enough, especially Greek in its spiritus asper which frequently proceeded from the digamma, and in English itself it is not quite without example. The most certain proofs are *to whoop* (also pronounced *hoop)* meaning to cry, make a noise, compared with the Gothic *vôpjan;* and *hoop* (meaning *ring),* which evidently is to be placed with MHD. *weif;* Gothic *vaip* (coronam). Then from this *hooden* for Woden comes *hoodening* the name of the custom, formed in exactly the same way as *maying* from *May…* [Here follows a description of the part taken by Robin Hood and Maid Marian in the Morris dance] … If *hooden* was the result of a corruption of *Woden,* then this same *Robin Hood,* by means of his name, which is only a further corruption of hooden [30] also carries us to Woden. The stories in circulation concerning him [Robin Hood] completely prove him to be a myth (*Mirror,* 20, p.189). Robin Hood is said to have been and to have lived in Sherwood Forest with his band an outlaw from the end of the twelfth to the middle of the thirteenth century. His true name is supposed to have been Robert Fitzoothes, Earl of Huntingdon … [Here follow various traditions relating to Robin Hood] … Among his comrades there are especially named, his mistress *Maid Marian, Friar Tuck* and *Little John* ; both England and Ireland are in contest as to the place of burial of the last named. The features here reported show plainly that, however historical a personage Robin Hood may have been, yet folk-tales have transferred to him incidents which originally belonged to another person living in tradition. The name *Hood,* which is supposed to be a corruption of *Fitzoothes,* takes us, as has been said, to Woden; this is most probable on account of his appearance in the Christmas and May customs, and as will appear, by the naming of the first of May as *Robin Hood's Day* … but besides the name *Hood,* his christian name *Robin* appears to me to be worthy of notice … [Here follow arguments connecting the name Robin with knecht Rupert, as already shown in the extract from Grimm, (*supra* p.92) … A comparison of the myths and customs of other Indo-Germanic peoples, in conjunction with solitary instances remaining with us, show undoubtedly, Woden to be the approaching summer, the glorious conqueror of winter … Exactly on the same day, the first of May, the Irish O'Donoghue on his white horse, rises out of the Lake of Killarney and makes his procession with his elfin band. We may undoubtedly, instead of the first named, put Woden, in regard to whom there is often a hint of the Devil; whether any connection can be shown between the name O'Donoghue and that of Woden, I leave to Keltic scholars to decide … [Kuhn then suggests St. George as another variant of Woden and ultimately drifts into the Vedas, where it is not necessary to follow him].

NORDDEUTSCHE SAGEN, MÄRCHEN UND GEBRÄUCHE *(A. Kuhn und W. Schwartz, Leipzig, 1848.)*

[Translation]

(p.369.) C. *Customs and Superstitions – Shrovetide.*

1. The Schimmel already described in the Customs of the Mark, is also found among the Shrovetide customs in several other districts of North Germany as far as Thüringia. To form the

figure a horse's head is often kept ready. To the lower jaw a string is fastened which the rider pulls, causing a clapping noise. In the neighbourhood of Köterberg near Höxter, a bear appears with the Schimmel.

Ibid. p.402, XI. *Christmas.*

125. The custom is wide spread among the country people throughout the whole of North Germany on Christmas eve, for a man to appear, bearded and covered with a great fur coat or concealed in pea haulm, who asks the children if they can say their prayers, and those who pass this test are presented with apples, nuts and peppercakes, but on the contrary, those who have not learnt to do so, are punished. In the Mittelmark the most wide spread name for him is *de hèle Christ* (der heilige Christ) or Knecht Ruprecht ; and Knecht Ruprecht (also Hans Ruprecht and verderbt Rumpknecht) in the district of Teupitz, Treuenbrietzen, Halle, in the golden Aue and Südharz; but in Mecklenburg on the contrary, he is called *rù Clas* or the rauhe *Clàs,* in the Altmark, Brunswick and Hanover as far as East Friesland, *Clas, Clawes, Clas Bùr,* and *Bullerclas.* Sometimes he carries a long staff and an ash bag, in Mellin for instance he has bells on his clothes; with the ash bag he beats the children, who cannot say their prayers, on account of which he is also called *Aschenclas*; sometimes, as for instance, at Otternhagen near Hanover, Deetz near Brandenburg, and Schorau near Zerbst, he rides round on a white horse in the manner which I have more than once described; not unfrequently he is accompanied by a Platzmeister [31]. At Hohennauen near Rathenow he appears accompanied by the so called Fays, that is to say men with blackened faces and dressed up in women's clothes; here, as at other places, as for instance, at Elm in Kl. Scheppenstädt and Cremlingen, there appears with him a so called *bear* which is covered with pea haulm and led on a long chain. In many places 'the holy Christ' (usually a maiden clad in white, who causes prayers to be said) and the Schimmelreiter appear as separate personages, as for instance, at Kemnitz near Treuenbrietzen; in Westphalia also, for instance at Bergkirchen and Basum in Osnabrück, the Schimmel appears at Christmas and New Year. At the last place it is called 'der spanische Hengst' (Spanish stallion).

126. In the Isle of Usedom on Christmas Eve, Ruprecht goes around and makes the children say their prayers. Three persons are comprised in this description; of whom, one carries a rod and an ash bag and is usually concealed in pea haulm; the second carries a so called Klapperbock, that is, a staff, over which a goatskin is stretched, with a wooden head, to the lower jaw of which a string is fastened running through the upper jaw and throat, so that if the bearer pulls the string, the jaws strike together with a clapping noise; the children who cannot say their prayers are pushed about with the Klapperbock ; at length, the third appears as Rider on a White Horse. As is general in the whole of Fore-Pomerania, Christmas presents are wrapped up in numberless coverings and thrown down before the door of the recipient with the cry, *Jùlklapp.*

WEIHNACHTEN, (*Professor Georg Rietschel. Velhagen und Klasing, Bielefeld und Leipzig. 1902*).

[Translation]

(p.108.) We have previously referred to the ride of Woden, who at this season flies through the air mounted on his white horse; the recollection of this is still preserved in many districts of Germany in the representation of the Schimmelreiter. Among the Wends of Neiderlausitz, in Silesia, Pomerania, Prussia, and other places, the Schimmelreiter comes at Christmas time into the spinning-room [32]. A young fellow, whose hat is drawn down well over his face, has tied on to him, behind and before, the rims of a sieve, which are covered with a linen cloth and represent the back of a horse. From the piece in front a rod sticks out, on which is fastened a horse's head made of tow, and enveloped in a white cloth, and at the back of the imitation horse there is a tail of tow or flax. The Schimmelreiter often jumps into the room over a chair placed at the door and seizes one of the assembled maidens for a dance. In Silesia, the Schimmel is represented by three young fellows, each of whom puts his arms on the shoulders of the one in front. All three are covered with a cloth. The foremost lad has an imitation horse's head tied on in front, or he merely holds out his hands, covered with a cloth, to represent the horse's head and neck. A fourth lad is seated as Rider on the shoulders of the middle one of the three lads who are covered with the cloth. The Schimmel without the Rider is also occasionally seen, but more often accompanied by a bear, a lad called the Erbsbär [33], who is concealed under pea haulm, plays the part of the chained bear. It is difficult to say what the origin of this may be. In some districts they are accompanied by the Haferbräutigam [34] or Habersack – a lad completely concealed in oatstraw. In the Isle of Usedom, there is the Klapperbock – a young fellow with a goat's head, the bottom jaw of which is moveable, and by means of a string, the two jaws can be knocked together, making a clapping noise. He pushes the children about who cannot say their prayers.

NIEDERSACHSEN [35] (Jahrgang VIII, Jan. I, 1903).

[Translation]

New Year's Customs in some Westphalian Villages on the Weser, by Heinrich Franke, Bückeburg.

(p.111) In the barn [36] of the village inn are collected figures, dressed up in a most peculiar fashion and carrying on all sorts of foolery. They are the young fellows of the village seeing the old year out. No one knows who any of the others are, for it is considered the proper thing to remain unrecognised so far as possible. Only the 'Wüder', as Wodan, or the Wild Huntsman, is known to all the others, for he has been chosen by the young men of the village, generally on the second day of the Christmas holidays. He sits at the table – his face blackened, and on his head a fur cap in which is a cock's feather. In his hand he holds a cow's horn, from which, from time to time he entices notes of a most unearthly kind, while his companions employ themselves cracking their long whips. Shortly before midnight, the Wüder gives a signal, and in an instant all is still as if by stroke of magic wand, then all leave the barn and before long have mounted their steed, which consists of a horse's head on a frame, over which hangs a white cloth – another moment of deep quiet, and then, all at once – a hullabaloo as if the earth would open, cracking of whips, prolonged blasts on the horn, dogs barking – and the phantom crew is seen galloping up and down the village road, until at length the Wüder and his band disappear into the farmhouse of some well-to-do peasant, who must stand treat to the wild troop. and if he does so to the satisfaction of the Wüder, then his house will be protected from all mischief. In the villages on the Weser this practice, which takes place on New Year's Eve, is called, for short, 'Schimmelreiten', it is however nothing else than an imitation of the Wild Huntsman, who, according to the old tradition, every year on New Year's Eve flies through the air with his band.

The similarity of the German custom of Schimmelreiten with the hooden horse is too obvious to require emphasis. The two principal features, which they have in common, are the horse, and the men dressed up in women's clothes; for we may not unreasonably compare die Feien who accompany the Schimmelreiter with the hoodeners' Mollie.

The German descriptions of the Schimmel are not very full, and it is difficult to form any exact notion in detail of the manner in which the horses' heads are made up; in some cases, it is not even said whether a real head or skull is used or not, but in Rietschel's *Weihnachten* (*supra* p.101) the horse's head is said to be made of tow. In Haupt's *Zeitschrift* (*supra* p.97), the description is merely 'a horse's head always kept ready for that purpose', though it is curious to note that the lower jaw of the horse's head is said to work with a string and make a snapping noise, yet this does not help us to determine whether it was a skull or a wooden head, for the real skull used in the Cheshire Souling custom is worked in the same way. In Germany we find, as is the case in England, that the horse, though most frequently, is not the only mimic animal associated with these customs, for example, the slaughter of the mimic ox in the Mittelmark at Shrovetide, as described in the *Märkische Sagen und Märchen* (*supra* p.96) and the Klapperbock custom in the Island of Usedom (*supra* pp.98, 100 and 101). The Klapperbock, being the mimic head of a goat, is expressly stated to be a wooden head over which a goatskin is stretched; the similarity of construction between the hooden horse and the Klapperbock is worth noting, the lower jaw of each being pulled with a string and making a snapping noise.

The German Schimmelreiter generally appears at Christmas-time, although, as is the case with several of the English customs described in Chapter IV, he sometimes appears at other seasons, such as Shrovetide and Whitsuntide, and even at festivals of indeterminate date, such as shooting competitions and even weddings.

There are characters which accompany the Schimmelreiter which do not appear to be represented in any of the English customs of this type, such as Knecht Ruprecht and the Christmann. The Erbsbär which is described (*supra* pp.98, 100 and 101) as a lad concealed under pea haulm, who plays the part of a chained bear, would appear to correspond to the 'Straw bear', of Whittlesey in Cambridgeshire, an account of which is given in *Folklore* xx, 201, where the straw bear is stated to be a man completely swathed in straw and led on a string.

Before proceeding to discuss the German customs described in the above extracts, the existence of similar customs in Scandinavia should be noted; in response to my enquiry Mr. W. A. Craigie (the well-known authority on Scandinavian folklore) has informed me that in Feilberg's *Jul*, [36] vol. I, p.204, there is an account of the Swedish custom of Staffan's Ride. It appears that both in Sweden and Norway it was the custom to ride out early in the morning of St. Stephen's Day, in order to water the horses at some particular place. In some places there was a race to get home first from the church. In Sweden, companies of young men went round singing Staffan's song, and Staffan himself was then provided with a horse consisting of two strong fellows tied together by a thong round the body; they hold short sticks in their hands, go on hands and feet and are concealed under a horsecloth. Among the company was also a 'Jule-buk' dressed in skin, his head consists of a carved goat's head, which he carries on a stick held in his hands. There was also a wether similarly dressed in skin and provided with a sheep's head. Apparently this custom still survives in some parts, or did till lately.

Although the similarity of the German custom of Schimmelreiten described in the above extracts, with our Kentish custom is self-evident, it must not be assumed, even if these customs have a common origin, that that common origin of necessity dates back to pre-Christian times, while our Saxon or Jutish forefathers were still in their homes on the continent. The earlier disciples of the Grimm school of folklore were accustomed to find in *Teutonic Mythology* the explanation and origin of all popular customs. This was especially the case in regard to such Christmastide customs as were not evidently of Christian origin. These non-Christian Christmas customs they held to be relics of an ancient pre-Christian Teutonic Yuletide Festival celebrated by our pagan ancestors at the time of the winter solstice. Sometimes their deductions were based on very slender grounds, and faint, if not forced, analogies, and have been adopted by more recent writers with little or no enquiry. We need therefore feel no surprise that they should connect Schimmelreiten with the memory of Woden, and in particular, of him as leader of the Raging Host; for, according to this school of thought, during the twelve days of Yuletide the god Woden, mounted on his eight-legged white horse Sleipnir, rushed through the air, followed by his raging host of warriors. After the introduction of Christianity the belief still lingered, though in a changed form, spectres taking the place of the god and his warriors; ultimately the myth took the shape of the Wild Huntsman, who rides through the air followed by a pack of hounds, and in this form, it was current during the middle ages throughout Scandinavia, Germany and England (and even parts of France); the names of various popular heroes, according to the locality, being identified with the character of the Wild Huntsman, such as Dietrich and Eckhart, and in England King Arthur and Herne the Hunter of Windsor. And according to Tylor's *Primitive Culture* (vol. I, p.278), Sir Francis Drake, in cottage tales, still heads the Wild Hunt over Dartmoor. In English folklore the Wild Hunt or Raging Host is supposed to be identified with the so-called 'Gabriel's Hounds'.

These are some of the reasons which are given for the theory that hoodening is a relic of our heathen Teutonic ancestors' worship of Woden; that this theory is correct I do not now say, for although this theory has my sympathy, yet it must be admitted that the evidence in support is not very strong; it may be correct, but one feels that the theory is based on inferences and analogies not strong enough for a foundation to carry the building erected on them. I do not so much question the connection of Woden with the traditions of the Raging Host, for on this point Grimm has given very strong authorities, but I do question the proof of any connection at all, between hoodening and the Raging Host or Woden. The extracts from German folklore before given, show that Kuhn, if he did not start, at any rate, was the first writer to elaborate, the theory connecting Woden with Schimmelreiten and the hooden-horse. Other German writers appear simply to have accepted Kuhn's theory without examining his arguments; for instance, Simrock, in his *Handbuch der deutschen Mythologie* (6th edit. 1887, p.230), after a brief mention of 'hoodening', merely expresses his agreement with Kuhn. It is therefore of great importance to consider Kuhn's arguments. The theory was first raised in the extract given from his 'Märkische Forschungen' (*supra* p.95), Kuhn's grounds for identifying Woden with the Schimmelreiter are there fully set out and should be referred to. His argument rests, first, on the assumption that Christianity is personified by the Christmann and heathendom by the Schimmelreiter, he then proceeds to assume the identity of Woden with the Rider 'because no one is better adapted to personify heathendom than the highest of the ancient gods'; so far, we have assumption pure and simple; nor do we find more satisfactory proof in the following details which he puts forward in corroboration:- (1) That die Feien (the

Fays), the men in women's clothes with blackened faces, are to be identified with the ancient Teutonic goddesses of Fate, and therefore are a link with Woden, with whom they chiefly connected; Kuhn, however, gives no real proof of the alleged identity between the goddesses of Fate and the Fays. (2) The presence of the White Horse (Schimmel) with which Woden is also associated. This again is not satisfying. (3) The date, i.e. the twelve nights of Yuletide, which are the festival of Frau Holla, with whom Woden stands in close connection, and therefore, Kuhn alleges, may well be the festival of the god also. I do not pursue this further, because Kuhn afterwards shows that the Schimmelreiter is not peculiar to the Twelve Nights, and besides, there are the views of Tille on this point, which will be more fully gone into. (4) The presence of Knecht Ruprecht, who, as well as Knecht Niclas, Kuhn states to be primitive house-sprites, but Tille [38] on the other hand, proves that Knecht Ruprecht (German Father Christmas), who has so long been thought to be the descendant of Wuotan Hruodperaht (Woden shining in glory), merely represents a type of a man-servant, and originally had nothing whatever to do with Christmas, and he shows that Knecht Ruprecht first made his appearance in a Christmas play in 1668.

In the next article (*Märkische Sagen und Märchen*, (*supra* p.101) Kuhn distinctly wavers in his opinion. In his own words, 'whether the Rider on a White Horse … is Woden as I assumed … I now leave undecided, for this figure has neither a precise name, nor are there existing, any special customs whatever which point to the acceptance of this theory'. He then states his only grounds for this conjecture are:- (1) The appearance of the Fays. (2) The form of the Rider in a broad brimmed hat and large cloak. (3) The peculiar punishment for those withdrawing from the wedding company.

It must be admitted that these reasons are not very impressing, and the reasons upon *which the third ground is based I am quite unable to follow.*

It is true, that in his article on Woden in Haupt's *Zeitschrift* (*supra* p.99), after his discovery of the account of the English customs in the *Mirror*, Kuhn returns with renewed and strengthened conviction to his theory, and arrives at two conclusions, namely: *(a)* that the word hooden in the expression hooden horse is to be derived from Woden, and that the practice of the custom is a relic of the worship of that god, and *(b)* that the custom of hoodening is connected with Robin Hood or, as Kuhn puts it, that the name (Robin) Hood is a corruption of hoodening.

As regards *(a)*, in spite of Kuhn's opinion, I think that the reasons I have put forward in the last chapter against the derivation of hooden from the name of the god Woden require explanation, before this derivation of the word can be accepted; and moreover, it will be seen that Kuhn bases his argument on the alternative name *wooden* horse, mentioned in the *Mirror* (*supra* p.30); but this loses point, when it is remembered that the expression wooden horse is merely the attempted explanation of hooden horse, given by educated people, because the head is *made of wood;* and this Kuhn did not know, for his knowledge of hoodening was restricted to the description in the *Mirror*, which does not contain any reference at all to the fact that the horse's head physically was wooden. With reference to Kuhn's conclusion that, apart from the word hooden being derived from Woden, the hooden horse custom as a relic of the worship of that god, this has been already fully discussed and his arguments considered, and I submit that no sufficiently convincing or satisfactory reasons have been given in proof.

As regards *(b)*, the connection between Robin Hood and the custom of hoodening must be apparent to anyone, who will take the trouble to read what has been recorded by various writers on the subject of the Robin Hood games and the Morris dance; and it is interesting to observe that Kuhn adopted this explanation in spite of the fact, that he had not before him, all the material which is before us; for, as before stated, it is evident that Kuhn's knowledge of the custom of hoodening was confined to the version in the *Mirror*, in which no mention is made of Mollie, whose presence with the hooden horse is, I venture to think, the strongest possible corroboration of the connection between the custom and Robin Hood. Kuhn assumes that the name (Robin) Hood is a corruption (Entstellung) of hooden; this, I submit, is putting the cart before the horse, the true explanation being that hooden is an adjectival form of the name Hood. It must not be overlooked that Kuhn endeavours to utilise the connection between the hooden horse and Robin Hood, merely, as a link in his chain of attempted proof of the connection between the hooden horse and Woden; to pursue this, he has to deny the actual existence of Robin Hood and summarily dismiss him as a mythological character, although, afterwards, he uses the rather contradictory expression, 'however historical a personage Robin Hood may be'. Much has been written on the question of whether Robin Hood actually existed. The *Encyclopaedia of National Biography* supports the mythological view, but in *Notes and Queries*, 7 Ser., Vol. III, there are a series of contributions indexed under the heading *Robin* Hood) in favour of his historical existence; and, on this point, the older writers may be consulted, such as Ritson and Gutch. Andrew Lang [39], speaking of Robin Hood, says 'Some of the learned mix him up with Woden, which seems a wild conjecture'.

There is among more modern German folklorists a reaction against attributing the origin of all popular customs to Teutonic mythology. Alexander Tille, in particular, has written two very interesting works, one in German – *Die Geschichte der deutschen Weihnacht,* Leipzig, 1893 – and the other in English – *Yule and Christmas, their Place in the Germanic Year,* London, David Nutt, 1899. In the latter work, more especially, he attacks the idea that there ever was, in pre-Roman times, any Teutonic midwinter festival, held at the time of our Christmas, and challenges the production of any evidence that the pre-Roman Germans had any knowledge of the winter solstice. Tille's theory is that the great winter festival of the ancient Teutons was originally on November 11 (Martinmas Day), in the form of a feast connected with the slaughtering of their cattle, which the approach of winter compelled them to kill. For, owing, to the economic conditions of those days, they were able to find food through the winter, only for the cattle required for breeding. As time went on, there was an increase in the quantity of hay produced, owing to improved cultivation of meadows, and thus, the great slaughter-time slowly advanced further into winter, to St. Andrew's Day (November 30), and later to St. Nicholas' Day (December 5).

Tille denies (*Yule and Christmas,* p.115) that the 'chthonic and wind-deities, Wodan, Holda, Perchta, did by preference hover about Christmas', he asserts that 'plain statistics show that they appear with about equal frequency at all seasons of the year', and 'that the Christmas rides of the Wild Huntsman and his host cannot be proved to be older than the sixteenth century'.

A writer in *The Church Times* (*supra* p.38), endeavours to connect the hooden horse with the practices (condemned in the Penitential of Archbishop Theodore) of those 'who on the kalends of January clothe themselves with the skins of cattle and carry heads of animals'; these practices, Tille says, 'are, as far as they appear in Old Gaul and the furthest west of Old Germany, in the form of a general masquerade, of Roman origin', but he draws a distinction between these practices and those of the Schimmelreiten type, as will be seen from the following passage:-

> The dressing up of artificial animals, however, which is found all over German soil, from Martinmas till mid-Lent – confined in olden days to the time about Martinmas, extended from the sixteenth century to about Christmas, and since then prolonged till mid-Lent – is a slaughtering custom, probably of purely Germanic growth. Originally the real animals destined to be killed were dressed up. whilst bye and bye, in part at least, artificial animals were placed in their stead. The domestic male animals which had been kept for stud purposes to the close of the season, were killed at the beginning of December – December 5th being, in ancient Tirol, the day for killing the boar. The slaughtering of these animals was a kind of public affair, since, wherever the *Mark-genossenschaft* existed, only one bull, one stallion, and one boar were kept for the whole community, so that those who, not being members of the community, wished to use the animal for their own herds had to pay extra for it.

If Tille's theory as to the origin of the artificial animal processions be correct, our hooden horse has indeed a humble ancestry, compared with a descent from Woden. It must be confessed, however, that his reasons for attributing the origin of the artificial animal processions to the ancient slaughter customs are not clear; one would rather be inclined to attribute that origin to those of the skull type, which Tille says are of Roman origin; and the pretended slaughter of the mimic ox, found among the Shrovetide customs in the Mittelmark, does not support Tille's view; for judging from the description given in his *Märkische Sagen und Märchen* (supra p.96), the mimic ox in question belonged to the artificial class and not to the skull type; but, as I have stated in Chapter IV, there may be no difference of origin between the two types.

The enquiry, to which this Chapter was stated to be restricted, has now been pursued as far as it profitably can be; and I fear that the answer to the question 'can we reasonably connect the ultimate origin of our custom with the ancient worship of our pagan Teutonic ancestors, and in particular, with the worship of Woden?' must be in the negative. I regret that I have no alternative theory to put forward as to the ultimate origin of the custom, except that the question seems of necessity involved with the origin of the hobby horse, and its first association with the Robin Hood games; for it may fairly be submitted that in the last Chapter good grounds were shown for attributing the proximate origin of the hooden horse to Robin Hood; and there one must leave it, for this present Chapter has shown that, in any endeavour to pursue the origin further, we become involved in a maze of unsatisfactory surmises. I regret that this Chapter should end in a cul-de-sac, but even that is better than evolving fantastic theories. Although my conclusions in any particular may be wrong, I venture to hope that the material I have collected together on this subject may assist some other enquirer to give us a more definite explanation of the ultimate origin of the Hooden Horse.

THE END

THE HOODEN HORSE

FOOTNOTES

1   But as to this see Chapter III.

2   The good old Kentish word 'ellinge' best describes it.

3   Sometimes a glossy black material (? holland) is used instead of sacking. This was so in the case of the Lower Hardres horse.

4   The Rider's military outfit of khaki clearly belongs to the post Boer War period, and certainly has nothing to do with our pagan ancestors.

5   J.V. von Scheffel's historical romance, *Ekkehard*, treats of Suabia in the tenth century, a time when heathen customs still largely prevailed in that part of Germany, notwithstanding that Christianity had obtained the upper hand. The incident referred to in the text is that related in Chapters VIII and IX of the book. Two of the characters, Audifax and Hadumoth, by accident and themselves unseen, are the observers of what the Author represents as a heathen ritual involving the eating of horseflesh. Shorn of literary embellishments, it may be shortly said that they are supposed to see – a slaughtered animal, a head like that of a horse nailed to a tree, bones, and a vessel containing blood, which is ceremonially sprinkled; and men drinking beer, also ceremonially. I do not think this assists us, in spite of the two common factors, the horse's head and the beer, which, admittedly, the hoodeners' drink, though not ceremonially. Moreover, one must not forget that von Scheffel in the same romance represents the Christmas tree, in its present form, as being a feature of German Christmas festivities in the tenth century, when, as a matter of fact, there is no record of the present-day Christmas tree in Germany before the beginning of the seventeenth century, in spite of the well-known picture of Christmas in Luther's Family.

6   As before stated this man is called the hoodener.

7   The Marie Llwyd referred to in pp. 34 and 35 and fully described in chapter IV.

8   See however the information as to Scandinavia obtained from Mr. W. A, Craigie, Chapter VI. *infra*.

9   Further information as to Ash-next-Sandwich will be found in Mr. G. C. Solley's statement in Chapter V.

10   It would be of interest to know the manner in which this song became connected with the hooden horse, for these verses appear to show an influence of the custom of wassailing the orchards, referred to in a contribution to *Notes and Queries* in 1852 (Ser. I, v. 293), and stated as being practised at Chailey in Sussex. It is called Apple-howling. A troop of boys visit the orchards and encircling the apple trees they repeat the following words:-

'Stand fast root. bear well top;
Pray the God send us a good howling crop:
Every twig, apples big,
Every bough, apples enow.
Hats full, caps full,
Full quarters, sacks full.'

11 The older people pronounced this name 'Winkit'.

12 This old lady survived in good health to see her hundredth birthday and Elham did honour to the occasion, and I am glad to say I kept the appointment. She died within the next fortnight.

13 Mrs. Clayson died in the summer of 1908.

14 I assure those interested in place names that this is a genuine name – in spite of its suspicious resemblance to the title of that charming child's book, *Jemima Puddleduck*. In the parish of Chislet there is another place called Puddledock or Nethergong.

15 I am told that *Folk-Lore and Folk Stories of Wales*, by Marie Trevelyan (Elliot Stock) 1909, also contains an account of the Mari Llwyd with a description of another horse-head custom called 'Aderyn Pig Llwyd' – the Bird with the Grey Beak – which appears to be almost identical with Mari Llwyd.

16 The reference to 'goodening' in this passage is inexplicable, goodening is a totally distinct matter, being the name given to the custom of soliciting alms by old women on St. Thomas' Day, and by no power of imagination can a horse's head, wooden or otherwise, have anything to do with that name.

17 There is *Waddenhall* Farm, in the Parish of Waltham, Kent, close to the historic Stone Street.

18 Verstegan, in his *Restitution of Decayed Intelligence* (1634) p.81, also derives Wood*nes*borough from Woden, but Verstegan is of course of no repute as an authority. The successful persistence, in writing, to the present day of the genitive form 'Woodnesborough' is to be noted, having regard to the footnote to p.159 of Grimm's *Teutonic Mythology*, Vol I. It must not be thought that 'Winsboro'' is merely a modern provincial corruption of Woodnesborough, it appears in the oldest records. In Hasted's *History of Kent* (1798), Vol. IV, p.230, we find, 'Woodnesborough, or Winsborough as it is usually called'. Harris, in his *History of Kent* (1719), p.238, says 'Wodensborough, or as 'tis now called Winsborow'; but Kilburne's *Kent* (1659) has 'Woodnesborough' only.

I have made notes on this point from a number of ancient title deeds, which I have inspected, relating to land in this parish, which may be worth recording. The form 'Woodnesborough alias Winsborough' occurs in six separate deeds, dated respectively, 1648, 1649, 1663, 1669, 1683, and 1696. Another deed, dated 1677, has 'Woodenburrough alias Winsborough', and another, dated 1648, has 'Winsborough alias Woodnesborough'. Going further back to 1630, 'Woodnesborow alias Winsborow', and in 1614, 'Woodnesborowe alias Wynnesborough', until, in a deed dated 1551, we find the one form 'pôcha de Wynsbrough'. I have not had access to private title deeds of earlier date, and for examples of the form of the name for the few next earlier centuries I can only quote the following, which occur in the series of Kent Fines, &c., reprinted in *Arch. Cant.* Proceeding backwards in order of date, we find: 'Wodenesburgh', – Assessment to Knight the Black Prince, 20 Edward III. (1346) *Arch. Cant.*, X, 120. 'Wodnesberg', 'Wodenesbergh', and 'Wodenesberghe', Kent Fines, 6 Edward II. (1313) ibid. XII, 289, XI, 353, 355, 357, and 'Wodnesbourghe', Holders of Fees in Kent, 38 Henry III. (1254) ibid. XII, 209. In these cases it will be noticed that the alternative form is not used, which is the more curious because in Domesday we find only 'Wanesberge'. Here I must relinquish the pursuit though it would be of interest to know in what form the name appears in Saxon times, but my enquiry in *Notes and Queries* has brought no reply.

19   One cannot imagine Queen Mary of Scotland herself taking a very austere view on the subject of these games.

20   Bishop Percy and Mr. Steevens agree in making Maid Marian the Mistress of Robin Hood. Gutch – *A Lytell Geste of Robin Hood*.

21   In the Tollett window this ladle is shown in the mouth of the hobby horse.

22   The well known iconoclast who in 1642 wrought destruction among the stained glass windows in Canterbury Cathedral.

23   But as to this see Tille's opinion in *Yule & Christmas* quoted in the next chapter.

24   From the German colloquial adage, 'Wenn meine alte Tante nur Räder hätte, dann wäre sie ein Omnibus'; the English equivalent assumes the possession of wings by pigs as a condition precedent to flying.

25   Clapping goat.

26   The writer's meaning being, I take it, that the correspondence between the German and the English customs shows a common Teutonic origin – this assumption, if proved, of necessity involving a hoary antiquity.

27   As to the explanation of the expression, wooden horse, see my remarks *supra* p.81

28   As regards Kent see *supra* p.82

29   It is of clear that 'hooden' is the adjectival form of Hood, and not that Hood is a *corruption* of hooden.

30   A man whose duty it was to make room for the performers and keep the crowd off.

31   Spinnstube means not only spinning room, but also the evening gatherings of the German peasant girls, who in the winter time, with their spinning wheels, visit the older married women in turns, in order to spin, tell stories, and meet their lovers. This practice has in some parts of Germany entirely disappeared, but still exists in remote mountain villages in Thüringia and the Black Forest. The clergy do not look on the custom with favour.

32   Pea-bear.

33   Oat-bridegroom.

34   A fortnightly folklore periodical.

35   *Die Scheune* can only be translated by 'barn', but in this passage it means more exactly *die Diele* (platt-deutsch *de Deel*). Every peasant house (including the village inn) in Niedersachsen has a wide open room or hall in the centre known as *die Diele*; on the one side of *Die Diele* are the doors of the living rooms, etc., and on the other side, the doors of the cowstalls, etc., all being under one roof. In the winter the corn is thrashed in *die Diele*, and here too, the young folks assemble to dance and play on the occasion of their merry-making.

36   This work was reviewed by Mr. Craigie in *Folklore*, XVII, p.366.

37   *Yule and Christmas*, p.116.

38   *Longman's Magazine*, July. 1900. p.286.

THE REVIVAL OF THE CUSTOM

THE HOODEN HORSE POST PERCY MAYLAM

An article by Dr Geoff Doel

In the short term, Percy Maylam's researches for his book and the enthusiastic interest he took in the custom led to both to its survival and its continuation for a while under the aegis of the Trice family, as well as the re-adoption of the Mollie into the Hooden Horse play at St Nicholas-at-Wade. The jockey Tom West was interviewed about this in old age by Simon Evans. He remembered the team touring venues in St Nicholas which included St Nicholas Court and The Bell Inn; in Sarre they visited Bolingbroke Farm, Sarre Court and The Crown Inn; and at Monkton, they took in Monkton Court, Gore Street Farm and The New Inn (now The White Stag). After a break of forty-five years, the Hooden Horse custom was revived at St Nicholas in 1966, featuring Waggoner, Mate, Farmer's Boy, Horse and Fiddler, with the addition of a village play, a new version of which is produced every year. As far as I am aware, this is the first example of a play being performed with the Hooden Horse.

William Castle (1875-1940), a farm labourer from Quex, was a member of the Acol Hoodeners until about 1925. An Acol Hooden Horse appeared at the Second World War victory celebrations in 1945, featuring one of the Laming Family (a family mentioned by Percy Maylam). This performance is a kind of missing link between tradition and revival. As indicated by the letter quoted in my introductory essay, and by other memories, hoodening survived longest at Deal, probably up until the mid-1930s, long enough to overlap with the first revival team at Balgowan School, Beckenham.

Percy Maylam's book and its clear photographs considerably heightened awareness of the custom and led to the identification and rescue of several authentic old Hooden Horses. St Nicholas-at-Wade has two old Hooden Horses. Dobbin, the main horse being used (and photographed) at St Nicholas in 1905 for Maylam's book, was rediscovered in 1965. It was given to the St Nicholas Hoodeners by Arthur ('Chip' or 'Chuck') Bolton, groom to Mr William Broadley, owner of St Nicholas Court and was thought to have been in the possession of the Trice family at the Court for 130 years. The second St Nicholas horse is called Black Beauty or Young Dobbin, and was found in a Canterbury antique shop in 1976, which in turn had bought it from the Post Boy Galleries, at Flimwell in Sussex.

An early revival team, The Wickhambreaux Hoodeners, have two horses dated between 1870 and 1900. The Swan Inn at Wickhambeaux was renamed The Hooden Horse in 1956. Later in the century there was briefly a chain of Hooden Horse pubs across Kent, but these have also sadly demised.

Maidstone Museum has two most interesting Hooden Horses which were found in a barn at Wingham, but are not currently on public display (though can be produced on request with advance notice), and are in a sad state of neglect. One is quite small (perhaps 3ft 6in with a fixed wooden pole) and could be for a juvenile. The horse has leather ears, the nostrils are cut out and the eyes indented, and it is painted black, red and white, with a blanket covering and a jaw that is pulled open and shut with a string. Stones are fixed in the jaw to create the snapping noise.

The second head seems to be full sized, but lacks its pole and its strings are broken. It also has stones for teeth and a horse brass on its forehead and a rosette. It has a studded belt and a mane of coloured streamers.

The Deal Maritime Museum also has two horses (formerly at Folkestone Library); one is the original, photographed by Maylam at Walmer, and the second is modern. The curator is helpful and approachable on information regarding these. There is a modern Deal Hoodeners team with a modern horse from about 1996, which continues the local tradition of using green sacking.

There has been a revival at Whitstable since the Second World War, where the horse is decorated with oyster shells. The present horse used by the Whitstable Hoodeners dates to about 1980, but has 'older trimmings'. The Jack in the Green Festival has also been revived (early May bank holiday) and the Hooden Horse can usually be seen there. Hop Hoodening is a modern September tradition, established in 1959, which features the Hooden Horse out of season, and the Tonbridge Hoodeners are sometimes to be seen at the Kent County Show (see back cover) or Kent folk festivals.

The Broadstairs Folk Festival has a Hooden Horse as its symbol, and the founder of the festival and English Folk Dance and Song Society, gold medallist Jack Hamilton, had a Hooden Horse made which is now in the possession of Nick Miller. Barnett & Olive Field, columnists and folk dance organisers, made a copy of the Deal Hooden Horse in 1953 which appeared at the Folkestone Coronation celebrations and at his dance events.

The Tonbridge Mummers and Hoodeners have been performing since 1981 a west Kent Hooden Horse Play, although admittedly the tradition appears to lie solely in the eastern part of the county. The play used by Tonbridge was written by myself and Nick Miller in 1981, and has elements drawn from associated horse-disguise traditions, and features the death, resurrection and prophetic powers of the horse for comic effect. In particular, we used bits from the *Comberbach Souling Play* from Cheshire and the *Symondsbury Play of Tommy the Pony* from Dorset, plus a large number of dreadful puns of our own invention. The revival of the horse is first attempted by a 'Horse Doctor', who pulls out a long string of 'guts', but eventually the gutless horse is revived by a Maiden's kiss ('to raise this horse to life and bliss'). I believe we borrowed the idea of the Maiden's kiss from Alan Austen's splendid West Malling Mummers; they have since borrowed the idea of the guts from us, which shows the inter-changeability of ideas which I'm sure occurred in the old days in local areas. Some of the new east Kent Hooden teams are remarkably similar to the Tonbridge one, and some people now regard it as part of the tradition. Several people have informed me that we couldn't have written the play because it is traditional! Others have told me that they were performing it before we wrote it! It's a fascinating example of the evolution of customs.

In west Kent, the earliest team to have a Hooden Horse may have been the Ravensbourne Morris in 1947, who may be featured in a mid-twentieth century photo showed in this book of a Hoodening Party wearing Morris bells. The Ravensbourne horse may have come from a Beckenham School horse used in the late 1930s. The Hartley Morris has a Hooden Horse as their totem animal, and Phil Burkin of the Hartley Morris made both the Hartley and the Tonbridge Hoodeners' horses, copied from Maylam's Walmer horse.

Other revival sides in east Kent include Sandling, Sandgate, the East Kent Morris Men, Birchington, and Chislet. Hooden Horse conventions are held every November, currently at Simple Simon's in Canterbury, but previously at the Marsh Gate Inn near Herne Bay, which has its own Hooden Horse dating from about 1900, found in a barn in Hoath in 1974. Chislet Hoodeners use this.

For a long period, Percy Maylam's book remained the only word on the Hooden Horse. Then in 1978, Dr E.C. Cawte set the Hooden Horse in a British context in his classic study *Ritual Animal Disguise* (Brewer, 1978) which was a great influence on so many of us. My wife Fran & I wrote a small book sponsored by South East Arts in 1992 called *Mumming, Howling and Hoodening: Midwinter Rituals in Sussex, Kent and Surrey* (Meresborough, 1992) which quoted extensively from Maylam and included some of his photos, plus some modern ones of my own. Our *Folklore of Kent* (Tempus, 2003) has a substantial section and photographs on the Hooden Horse. On the education front, I have lectured extensively on the Hooden Horse over the past thirty years on my Folklore & Traditional Culture courses at Goldsmith, Birkbeck & Morley Colleges and the City Lit. in London and for the University of Kent, the WEA and Historical & Archaeological Societies. All this would not have been possible without Percy Maylam's researches, book and photographs. Many years ago I supplied the English Folk Dance and Song Society with a photocopy of Maylam's rare book (I think they have their own copy now!). There is a very useful website by Ben Jones of the St Nicholas Hoodeners on 'Hoodening History', which uses Maylam extensively but which also provides most valuable information on Thanet post First World War survivals, and on the Thanet revivals after the Second World War, featuring some original photographs.

Thus Percy Maylam's vision of both documenting and preserving the custom has proved successful, and his book has been the major factor both in disseminating knowledge of the tradition and in enabling its revival. Percy Maylam also correctly saw it as a distinctive east Kent custom, like Gavelkind, and he saw ahead to a time when regional culture would once again be important. Over the past ten years or so, I have found much more interest in distinctive local traditional culture (hop-picking being another example) rather than national, and the Hooden Horse revival has benefited from this. Percy Maylam's original book only had 303 copies and is both desperately rare and desperately sought after. A new edition is much needed and I am most grateful to the Maylam family for supporting this, in particular Richard Maylam, Percy's great nephew and one of my co-editors. Richard is a leading light in the Society of Men of Kent and Kentish Men, who have loyally supported and sponsored the Tonbridge Hoodeners at events and talks for many years. My other co-editor is Mick Lynn, the Doctor in the Tonbridge Hoodeners, and thus a key figure in reviving! He also combines this with the even longer tradition of the Musician in the Hooden Horse party, and is very relieved that Percy belatedly changed his mind in realising the importance of this figure.

So Hoodeners everywhere, raise your glasses to the memory of Percy Maylam, 'a good man who did good things'.

SHORT BIBLIOGRAPHY

FOR THE TWO HOODEN HORSE ARTICLES BY GEOFF DOEL

Cawte, E.C., Ritual Animal Disguise, Ipswich: Brewer, 1978

Doel, Fran & Geoff, *Folklore of Kent*, Stroud: Tempus, 2003,
   Re-issued Stroud: The History Press, 2009

Doel, Fran & Geoff, *A Kent Christmas*, Stroud: Sutton, 1990, 1998

Doel, Fran & Geoff, *Mumming Hoodening & Howling – Midwinter Rituals in Sussex, Kent
   & Surrey*, Rainham: Meresborough, 1992

Hutton, Ronald, *The Stations of the Sun*, Oxford: OUP, 1996

Maylam, Percy, *The Hooden Horse – An East Kent Custom*, Canterbury, 1909

THE CUSTOM OF GAVELKIND IN KENT

By Percy Maylam

All freehold land of socage tenure in the County of Kent is subject to the Custom of Gavelkind, and all land in Kent is presumed to be subject to the Custom unless the contrary be proved. The term 'land' is here used in its technical meaning and includes not only the surface but all above and below the surface, such as houses and minerals.

It is proposed to state as concisely as possible the incidents of the Custom – those which have become obsolete as well as those now in effective force – for matters of antiquarian interest must be dealt with to a certain extent, in order that the present incidents of the Custom may be properly understood, and therefore as a preliminary, it is necessary to give a very short description of 'Tenures'.

TENURES

'Tenure' of land is founded upon feudal principles and implies the doctrine, which still prevails, that all land belonging to a subject must be holden of some superior, and either mediately or immediately of the sovereign. This is so even in the case of what is popularly regarded as absolute ownership namely – a fee simple. An owner of such an estate is *tenant* in fee simple, holding either of the sovereign directly or of some intermediate lord. Usually, in such a case the doctrine has no appreciable effect, except in the case of a freehold tenant of a manor paying a small quit rent. This is the sense in which the word 'tenant' is used throughout this sketch.

After the feudal system had become established in this kingdom, there were two main divisions of lay tenures – (1) FREE and (2) BASE or servile (now represented by copyholds).

We need only concern ourselves with free tenures which were subdivided into (a) KNIGHT SERVICE, otherwise called tenure by chivalry, and (b) *FREE SOCAGE*.

The distinction between the two kinds of free lay tenures being, that *Knight service* was of a purely military character, and the services to be rendered to the superior lord were honourable, but uncertain in respect of quantity and the time of rendering them. Free socage was a non-military tenure, the personal services to be rendered by the tenant were chiefly of an agricultural character, and the money payments were certain and fixed. The term 'socage' has been derived from the Saxon word 'soc' meaning a liberty or privilege, and also from the same word in French, meaning a ploughshare. In its widest sense free socage denoted a tenure, for which the services to be rendered were not only honourable but also certain and fixed.

The hardships connected with the tenure of knight service were so oppressive that on the Restoration, by the Act 12 Charles II cap.24, it was turned into free socage.

There remains one other tenure to be mentioned – Tenure in FRANKALMOIGN or free alms, which occurred when a religious corporation held lands, the services for which (before the Reformation) were undefined, such as to pray for the souls of the donor.

GENERAL

The term 'Gavelkind' is used throughout this sketch to denote *the whole body of customs, which, under this denomination, are attached to freehold lands of socage tenure in Kent*. It is true that the term is also used at the present day to denote the custom of equal division among male heirs, which exists in certain definite localities in some other counties (although except in Kent it does not prevail throughout an entire County) but this usage of the term would appear to be by way of analogy, drawn from the predominant feature of the Kentish Custom: at any rate there is no record of the term 'Gavelkind' being applied to lands outside Kent, until the Act 31 Henry VIII cap.3.

There are two explanations given as to the meaning of the word 'Gavelkind'. One version says the word means 'give all kind' i.e. to all the male children: the other derives the word from 'gafol' meaning rent, in reference to the fixed rent and services rendered in respect of socage lands. Anyone who reads what Somner has written will have little doubt that the latter explanation is correct.

An important feature of the Custom is that while the existence of all other local customs has to be strictly proved in legal proceedings, in the case of Gavelkind it is sufficient to prove that the lands in question are situate in Kent, and then, the existence of this Custom is assumed without proof. In fact it was decided in 1902 in the case of *in re* Chenowith, Ward *v.* Dudley that Gavelkind is the common law of the land in Kent and not merely a custom contrary to the common law of the kingdom.

Therefore in regard to equal division among the male heirs, not only is it not necessary to prove equal partition in the past, but even the proof that a man and his ancestors have time out of mind inherited socage lands in Kent by descent to the eldest son, would not prevail against the custom of equal division; for Gavelkind is the 'Common Law of Kent'.

The more orderly method would be to deal with the subject chronologically, and in the first place to trace the origin and development of the Custom, but as the object of this sketch is more especially a practical one, it is proposed at once to set out the special incidents of the Custom. These were formerly more interesting and valuable than they are at present, but even from a practical point of view the obsolete incidents of the Custom are worth consideration, because, as will be seen, in most cases they have become obsolete, not by reason of their having been abolished, but because the privileges they embodied – once peculiar to the County of Kent, have been extended to the rest of the kingdom.

INCIDENTS OF THE CUSTOM
WHICH HAVE BECOME OBSOLETE.

(1) (a) Disputes as to ownership of Gavelkind lands were tried not by a Grand Assize of twelve knights, but by a jury of twelve men who were tenants in Gavelkind. (b) It would appear that trial by Wager of Battle, now altogether obsolete, was never applicable to Gavelkind lands. (c) There was also a special writ of 'gavelet' applicable to the case of a lord proceeding against a tenant in Gavelkind on default. These matters are to a great extent of antiquarian interest only and most obscure, and this was especially so in regard to the writ of gavelet, concerning which Robinson says "the rule was expressed in a Kentish dialect of which the clerks compiling the record were ignorant."

(2) In ancient times the general law was, that a man could not dispose of his freehold lands by will, but the owner of Gavelkind lands could do so by virtue of the Custom, and the power to devise by the custom seems to have applied in Kent to lands held by knight service as well as to lands held by socage. By two Statutes of general application passed in the reign of Henry VIII owners of socage lands were empowered to devise the whole of their lands, but owners of knight service lands only two thirds. All knight service tenures were abolished by 12 Charles II cap. 24, since when all owners in fee simple have the power to dispose of all their lands by will.

(3) In the days when the general law was, that on attainder for felony the lands of the person attainted were forfeited to the crown, lands held under the Custom were not subject to this rule (except in the case of treason), the maxim being 'the father to the bough, the son to the plough'. In 1870 an Act was passed abolishing forfeiture altogether, so that this privilege is no longer peculiar to Gavelkind.

It will be observed and may be here repeated that although the incidents before mentioned are no longer peculiar to the Custom, this has arisen, not by abolition, but because the privileges have been extended to the rest of the kingdom.

(4) There is one feature of the Custom, which is not obsolete in the sense that it is still the law, but it is obsolete in the sense that nowadays it is seldom used, that is the right of an infant owner (male or female) of Gavelkind lands, when of the age of 15 years, to sell and transfer his or her lands by feoffment (the ancient mode of conveying by means of symbolical delivery). Certain requirements have to be observed, so that the interests of the infant are protected. At one time this right was very valuable, but now the sale in most cases would be carried out by other procedure, the result of recent legislation.

INCIDENTS OF THE CUSTOM WHICH STILL EXIST
IN FULL FORCE, AND ARISE IN EVERY DAY PRACTICE.

(5) DOWER is the interest which the wife takes in the freehold lands of inheritance of her deceased husband, which any issue by her might possibly have inherited (but in the case of dower such issue need not have been born) and so far as he has not disposed of such lands by his will. The differences between the general law and the Custom in this respect are as follows:-

DOWER (GENERAL LAW).	DOWER (GAVELKIND).
A life interest in one *third* of such lands.	A life interest in one *half, so long as she remains chaste and unmarried.*

(6)   TENANCY BY THE CURTESY is the interest the husband takes in freehold lands of inheritance of his deceased wife, so far as they are not disposed of by her will. In the general law this is called 'Tenancy by the Curtesy of England', in Gavelkind it is termed 'Tenancy by the Curtesy according to the Custom of Gavelkind'. The differences between the two are:-

TENANCY BY THE CURTESY OF ENGLAND (i.e. GENERAL LAW).	TENANCY BY THE CURTESY ACCORDING TO THE CUSTOM OF GAVELKIND.
A life interest in *all* such lands of his deceased wife *provided he had issue by her born alive during the marriage capable of inheriting.*	A life interest in one *half* of such lands of his deceased *wife whether issue born or not, but so long only as he remains unmarried.*

(7)   On the death of a landowner intestate, according to the general law the eldest son takes all the landed property to the exclusion of the younger children, but according to our Custom the sons take equally between them, the customary rule applies also to the case of collaterals – for instance if brothers, uncles or cousins were the nearest male heirs, they would take equally and not the eldest alone. See the case of *in re* Chenowith before referred to.

Lands In Kent To Which The Custom Applies.

The Custom attaches to all lands held by tenure of free socage, and it is presumed to attach to all freehold lands in Kent, unless it can be shown that the land comes within one of the three exceptions next mentioned, always remembering that the presumption is in favour of the Custom applying, unless the contrary be proved. It may be here mentioned that an ordinary freehold rent charge, issuing solely out of Gavelkind lands, is subject to the Custom in the same way as the land; but the modern rent charge in lieu of tithes (when in the hands of a lay owner) issuing out of Gavelkind lands is not subject to the Custom.

The Custom does not apply to:-

(a)   Lands *originally* held by the tenure of knight service.

(b)   Lands *originally* held by the ecclesiastical tenure of frankalmoign (free alms).

(c)   Lands which have been disgavelled by Act of Parliament.

In order, however, to bring any particular case within exceptions (a) or (b), it must be shown that the land in question was at the time of the Conquest, held by the tenure of knight service or frankalmoign, as the case may be; and to prevent the operation of the

Custom, it is not sufficient to prove, that at some later date the land was held by one or other of these tenures. For instance, if land originally of socage tenure escheated to the Crown and were granted afresh by tenure of knight service or frankalmoign, the Custom would still attach notwithstanding. The converse rule also applies.

As regards exception (c), at various times, Acts of Parliament have been passed by which the lands of certain persons specified in the Acts were disgavelled. These disgavelling Acts were seven in number, the first being in the eleventh year of Henry VII, and the last being in the twenty-first year of James I (i.e. 1624). Although the wording of the disgavelling Acts was general, yet by judicial decisions their effect was restricted to the abolition of the incident of equal division among the male heirs, and the other incidents of the Custom remain.

None of these disgavelling Acts contained any schedule or description of lands disgavelled, beyond the general description of lands then belonging to the specified person or persons. So that at the present day, in order to bring any particular parcel of land within the operation of any disgavelling Act, it is necessary to show, that at the very time of passing the Act, it belonged to the particular person whose lands were disgavelled (proof that it so belonged before or after would not suffice). Any one acquainted with the difficulty of proving identity of parcels of land will realise how hopeless the task is of doing so, after 300 years, and consequently for all practical purposes these disgavelling Acts might never have been passed, owing to the legal presumption in favour of the Custom. In fact, in regard to all three exceptions, it may be confidently said that there is scarcely a legal practitioner in the County, who has ever known of a case where in actual practice the presumption in favour of the Custom has been rebutted; this is said with all respect to the learned author of the 'Tenures of Kent'.

ORIGIN OF THE CUSTOM.

If it be asked, how does it come that Kent possesses privileges not extended to other counties, one can give the popular explanation that the Conqueror conceded their ancient customs to the County of Kent, owing to their sturdy resistance: the story is told by Lambarde (who calls to witness 'Thomas Spot a monk and chronicler of St. Augustine's at Canterbury') that after the defeat of Harold, the common people of Kent took their weapons and met at Swanscombe, each man with a green bough, so that the Conqueror, on his approaching them, thought it was some miraculous wood that moved towards him, but they, casting their boughs from them, sounded the trumpet and showing their weapons, sent him a message offering him the choice of either peace or war, – peace, if he permitted them to enjoy their ancient liberties, or war, and that most deadly, if he denied them. The story goes on that William wisely chose peace and Kent retained its ancient liberties.

This version to some extent received judicial approval in the case of Doe d. Lushington v. Bishop of Llandaff. However this may be, the principle of equal division among the male heirs prevailed generally throughout the kingdom for some time after the Conquest; indeed it is questionable whether, even in the case of the tenure of knight service, the principle of primogeniture came into force until the reign of Henry I, and it was not until the reign of Henry III that primogeniture became the general law of the kingdom in regard to free and common socage lands. Therefore Kent, where the equal division of these lands among the male heirs is still the rule, is merely retaining a principle, which prevailed throughout the whole Kingdom long after the Conquest. Probably the same explanation applies to the other incidents of the Custom. It may be, that the small number of owners in Kent, who held land by the tenure of knight service, and the large number of those who held by the socage tenure, account for this. The small number of tenures in Kent held by knight service is very plainly evidenced by two Acts passed in the reign of Henry VI in connection with Actions of Attaint. Actions of Attaint were proceedings in the nature of appeal from the alleged false verdict of a jury. A statute passed in 1436 (15 Henry VI cap. 5) governed the procedure of these actions, and provided incidentally, that the Sheriff, in impanelling the jury to try an action of this kind, should not summon (among other persons exempted) tenants in gavelkind. Apparently this did not work, for we find that three years afterwards (1439), an Act was passed (18 Henry VI cap 2), which after referring to the Act of 1436, states 'seeing within the County of Kent there be but 30 or 40 persons at the most, which have any lands or tenements out of the tenure of gavelkind, because the greater part of the said County, or well nigh all, is of the tenure of gavelkind' and proceeds to remove the exemption conferred on gavelkind tenants.

OBJECTIONS ALLEGED AGAINST THE CUSTOM.

It is now right to consider the reasons, which have been put forward by those, who in the past, have desired to abolish the Custom.

In 1828 a Royal Commission was appointed to enquire into the Law of England respecting Real Property; one of the matters gone into by the Commissioners was the Custom of Gavelkind. The Appendix to the First Report (1829) contains the evidence of certain persons relative to the Custom, and pages 8 to 12 of the Third Report (1832) contain the Report of the Commissioners on the subject, the Appendix to the Third Report also contains some further evidence on this subject. The evidence on this particular matter has to be searched out, as it is embodied in a mass of material dealing with other subjects. The Commissioners recommended the total abolition of the Custom, and consequently in 1836 a Bill was introduced into Parliament for that purpose. The indignation aroused in Kent by this Bill was so great, that the Bill was withdrawn. Anyone who has the curiosity and patience to peruse the local papers of that day will find records of public meetings of protest.

It is of course of great importance to consider this adverse report, and also the evidence upon which it was founded, in two respects, (a) the grounds of objection, and (b) as to the capacity of those giving adverse evidence, to judge of the working of the Custom in every-day practice, for there will be experienced difficulty in doing justice to the reasoning of the Commissioners in arriving at (a) unless (b) is explained.

As regards Dower and Tenancy by the Curtesy, the Commissioners referred to the recommendations they had made for alterations in the general law on these matters (but their recommendations on these particular points have never been carried out), and they said that the expediency of preserving Gavelkind must rest upon its peculiar rule of descent.

(A) THE GROUNDS GIVEN BY THE COMMISSIONERS FOR RECOMMENDING THE ABOLITION OF THE CUSTOM.

(1) The Gavelkind rule of descent …if allowed to take effect independently of settlements and wills, must, in a few generations break down ancient families, and cause a sub-division of land unfavourable to agriculture and to every sort of improvement.

This of course is a finding pure and simple in favour of the feudal rule of primogeniture, and there is little doubt, but that this was the real ground at that date, of objection to the Custom. One witness, Mr. Taunton, K.C., speaking of the Custom said 'If it were more prevalent, its consequences would be extremely injurious under our monarchial form of government, which in my judgment cannot subsist without the right of primogeniture.' The witness apparently thought that the fact of all the sons of a small Kent yeoman, sharing their father's 20 acres, would instil seditious thoughts into the minds of the sovereign's younger sons against their eldest brother!

(2) That Gavelkind descent was generally controlled by settlements and wills, which shows that in truth, it did not peculiarly suit the necessities and inclinations of the owners of the soil.

By the same process of reasoning the Commissioners might with equal force have found, that, because there are more people who make wills than who die intestate, that the rules as to distribution of intestates' estates generally, does not suit the requirements of the kingdom. Moreover it must be said (without admitting the conclusion arrived at) that objection No. 2 rather takes away the effect of objection No. 1, for it is well-known that in practice, estates which are kept in the family for generations, are so kept, not by means of the rule of primogeniture, but by settlements made in every generation, and therefore, the chief, if not the only effect of the primogeniture rule, is felt where it is not wanted – in the case of the small freeholder, who has not the slightest thought of founding a family estate, and in whose case such a desire would be absurd. In justice to the large landowners of Kent – the landed gentry of ancient family, who not improperly may wish to hand down intact to their descendants, the estates which they themselves have so inherited, – one must say, that they, on previous occasions when the Custom of Gavelkind has been attacked, have disregarded, what, in theory, might be considered the interest of their class, and have championed the privileges of the whole County as sturdily as any.

(3) The gavelkind rule of descent had neither the advantage of primogeniture nor of equal partibility (meaning that the daughters are not included).

This objection is by far the most reasonable, the answer however is apparent, – if a Bill were introduced, abolishing the Custom of Gavelkind, as part of a general scheme for making landed property on death of an owner intestate, divisible among the next of kin, as in the case of personal property, then the supporters of the Custom might be put on their defence, but until this is done, they can say in reply to this objection – 'half a loaf is better than no bread', in other words, it is better that the sons should share equally (although the daughters are excluded), than that the eldest son should take all.

(4)   That owing to the splitting up of estates among a number of heirs, great inconvenience and expense was caused, especially where the deceased owner was a Trustee and his co-heirs were infants.

This objection has now ceased to have any force whatever, for by the Conveyancing Act 1881, all trust estates vest directly in the executor or administrator, and not the heir, and by the Land Transfer Act 1897, this is so in all cases, consequently there is no greater difficulty or expense in dealing with gavelkind land on death, than is now presented -by the general law, in regard to leasehold property, which vests in the executor or administrator for distribution among the next of kin.

(5)   There appeared to be a growing danger of questions arising as to what lands in Kent are exempt from the Custom of Gavelkind.

This objection deals with the three exceptions to the rule of presumption in favour of gavelkind. The report was made 80 years or more ago, and the 'growing danger' predicted by the Commissioners has not occurred; on the contrary, during the period between the date of the Report and the present day, it has become more and more unusual, for an attempt to be made to set up one of the three exceptions, i.e., that the land was originally of knight service tenure or frankalmoign or has been disgavelled. The probability, in the case of any legal practitioner in the County, nowadays, is that he has never *in actual practice*, known of a case where the presumption in favour of the Custom has been successfully rebutted, although the profession in the County are quite conversant with the information contained in Elton's *Tenures of Kent.*

(6)   There was nothing in the situation or circumstances of the County of Kent which rendered the Custom peculiarly adapted to that district.

This conclusion of the Commissioners can only have been arrived at, by reason of the class of witnesses, whose evidence was taken by them, of which more hereafter. As a matter of fact, there are in Kent and always have been, a very small number of very large landowners, and a very large number of very small landowners. The only statistics which the writer can conveniently consult, are contained in the [New] Domesday Book of Kent 1877, extracted from a return made to the House of Commons in 1876, from which it appears that in that year the total number of landowners in the County (outside the Metropolis) was 34,683, of which number 32,562 owned less than 50 acres each. Do not these figures speak for themselves? At that date only three persons owned more than 10,000 acres each.

The doctrine of equal division among the male heirs, is eminently more suitable than primogeniture, in a district containing so many small owners, for it is among this class that cases of intestacy usually occur, not among the larger owners.

(B) THE CAPACITY OF THOSE GIVING EVIDENCE BEFORE THE REAL PROPERTY COMMISSIONERS TO JUDGE OF THE WORKING OF THE CUSTOM.

The persons who were examined by the Commissioners consisted almost exclusively of Conveyancing Counsel practising in London. These gentlemen were doubtless selected from among the most able and learned men of their day, but it is evident, that this class could not have seen the ordinary every day working of the Custom of Gavelkind, they only saw, the abnormal and exceptional points, which presented difficulties to the Solicitor in the course of his every day practice, and on that very account came before Counsel, and doubtless it was upon the experience they had of such unusual points that their hostile opinion was founded. The persons, who did see the normal and usual working of the Custom of Gavelkind, as it presented itself in every day practice, were the Solicitors then practising in Kent, and it is in the highest degree noteworthy, that not a single Kentish Solicitor appears to have given evidence on the question, or have been asked by the Commissioners for his opinion.

REASONS FOR RETAINING THE CUSTOM.

In view of what has been written, these reasons may be shortly summarised as follows:-

(1)   The incidents of the Custom are fairer than the corresponding rules of the general law, and if any alteration be necessary, it is the general law that should be amended.

(2)   The incidents of the Custom are adapted to the requirements of small owners (of whom there are so many in Kent) and at the same time, do not practically affect the interests of the larger owners injuriously.

(3)   The incidents of the Custom which arise on an intestacy, occur much oftener than is usually supposed. In Kent, (or at any rate in East Kent), out of every three persons who die, leaving property of sufficient amount to require grant of Probate of their Wills or Letters of Administration to their Estates, two of such persons leave wills, and one dies intestate, and of course, as a rule, it is the small owner, and not the large owner, who leaves no will. It must also not be forgotten that although a will be left, the testator, owing to various causes, may, in the events which happen, die intestate as to portion of his property; this is not of infrequent occurrence, and then the Custom operates on the property not dealt with by will.

(4)   The grounds, formerly given for the abolition of the Custom, have, either been removed, or are not substantiated by the experience of actual practice. Notwithstanding, if the possibility of uncertainty as to tenure, is still felt to be an objection, on account of lands which may originally have been held by knight service, frankalmoign, or have been disgavelled, then it would be fairer to effect the desired uniformity, by enacting that all these lands should be subject to the Custom.

(5)   The Custom of Gavelkind is not a local custom (in the legal sense), but a part of the Common Law of England applicable to Kent, and needless interference by the legislature with an ancient custom, is to be deprecated; all new legislation, even if necessary, brings uncertainty, loss, and lawsuits. Especially in dealing with the rights of small landowners, is unnecessary alteration to be avoided, for it would take years and years before any alteration would be realized by this class, and in the meantime much hardship and injustice would be experienced.

(6)   Whatever may be the merits of the Custom, its existence does not injuriously affect the rest of the kingdom, its existence or abolition is a question domestic to the County of Kent, and consequently if the County be satisfied, the privileges of the County should not be interfered with in an arbitrary manner.

(7)   The Custom of Gavelkind has been handed down from father to son in the County of Kent from a time beyond the period of legal memory (i.e. 1189). It did not derive its origin from any Act of the legislature, because it existed before there was any Parliament. The earliest written record of the Custom goes back to the twenty-first year of the reign of 'King Edward the sonne of King Henrie', that is, the twenty-first year of Edward I., (A.D., 1293), when the Custumal of Kent is supposed to have been allowed by the Justices in Eyre in Kent; but the Custumal was not the origin of the Custom, it merely recorded 'Ces sont les vsages de Gauylekend e de Gauylekendeys en Kent, que furent deuant le Conquest, e en le Conquest, e totes houres ieskes en ca' (These are the usages of Gavelkind and of Gavelkind men in Kent, which were before the Conquest, and at the Conquest, and ever since till now).

Now once again our Custom is threatened. Clause 33 of the Real Property Bill 1913, (introduced into the House of Lords by the Lord Chancellor and withdrawn with the intention of being reintroduced next Session) provides for the total abolition of the Custom of Gavelkind. What are the reasons now alleged for desiring to abolish the Custom? Were our Parliamentary Representatives previously consulted?

It now behoves Men of Kent and Kentish Men, if they desire to keep the rights handed down to them by their fathers, to bestir themselves as in the like case their fathers ever did.

PERCY MAYLAM,
Canterbury
October, 1913

BIBLIOGRAPHY FOR GAVELKIND

A PERAMBULATION OF KENT by William Lambarde (containing the Customs of Kent). First edition 1576. Second edition 1596. Third edition (undated). Fourth edition 1640. Fifth edition 1656. Sixth edition 1826.

A TREATISE OF GAVELKIND by William Somner. First edition 1660. Second edition 1726.

THE HISTORY OF GAVELKIND with the etymology thereof by Silas Taylor. 1663.

TILE COMMON LAW OF KENT; or, the Customs of Gavelkind by Thomas Robinson First edition 1741. Second edition (a reprint of the original edition) 1788. Third edition 1822. Fourth edition, edited by J. D. Norwood, Solicitor of Ashford, 1858. Fifth edition, edited by C. I. Elton and H. J. H. Mackay, 1897.

REPORTS BY TILE COMMISSIONERS APPOINTED TO ENQUIRE INTO THE LAW OF ENGLAND RESPECTING REAL PROPERTY, 1829–1832.

First Report, 1829. Evidence in appendix.

Third Report, 1832, pp.8–12; And Evidence in appendix.

AN ADDRESS TO THE FREEHOLDERS OF KENT issued by the Kent Law Society 1836. Reprinted 1907.

This was first issued in consequence of the Bill introduced in 1836 for the abolition of the Custom in consequence of the Report of the Real Property Commissioners. The address is temperate and unargumentative, merely setting forth the advantages and disadvantages of the Custom, leaving the decision to those interested. In the end, such opposition was shown to the proposed abolition that the Bill was withdrawn.

CONSUETUDINES KANCIÆ; a History of Gavelkind by Charles Sandys (a Canterbury Solicitor) 1851.

This contains a copy of the Custumal of Kent alleged to have been allowed by the Justices in Eyre in the 21st year of Edward I.

THE TENURES OF KENT by C. I. Elton, 1867.

This work contains a vast amount of learning, the author's object was 'to show how much less land in the county is of the nature of Gavelkind than has been commonly presumed'. However accurate the author's views may be in theory, in actual practice the operation of the Custom has not been restricted.

NOTE – Both Mr. Norwood's edition of Robinson and Sandy's Consuetudines Kanciæ were allowed to be cited as authorities in the case of Maskell and Goldfinch, 1895, L.R. 2 Ch. 525.

INDEX

Abbot's Bromley Morris dance, 75, 76, 85, 87, 89, 98

Acol, 17, 36, 46, 48, 49

Aderyn Pig Llwyd, 108

Altmark, 96, 97, 100

Alphabet of Kenticisms (Pegge), 11, 27

Antiquary, The, 38, 79

Arch. Cant., 27, 90, 108

Ashford, 55

Ash-next-Sandwich, 16, 42, 51, 83, 91, 107

Aspirate, 44, 82

Betteshanger, 49

Birchington, 17, 36, 45, 46, 48, 112

Blackened, faces of hoodeners sometimes, 14, 78, 89, 98, 100, 101, 104

Blackmore Country, The, 76

Blean, 52

Book of The Beginnings, A (Massey), 34, 43, 81, 93

Book of Christmas, The (Hervey), 30

Book of Days (Chamber) 87, 90

Bosholders, 37

British Goblins (Sykes), 78

Broad Oak, 52

Bromley Record, The, 36

Bull hoodening, 79, 80, 106

Burbage (Wilts), 79

Canterbury, 7, 16, 25, 52, 53, 56, 90

Carmarthenshire, 78

Carol singing and hoodening, 33, 35, 41, 42, 47

Caytis, 24

Chartham, 21, 53, 54

Cheshire (Ormerod), 79

Cheshire Souling, 14, 15, 78

Chislet, 38, 51

Christmann, der, 94, 95, 102, 103

Christmas Bull, 79

Christmas horse, 54

Christmasse, A Righte Merrie (Ashton), 39

Christ-puppe, die, 94, 95

Church Times, The, 17, 37, 39, 40, 43, 78, 82, 105

Cleve (Monkton), 48

Combmartin, 76

Common Law, 115, 123

Concert Room, &c., Anecdotes (Busby), 29, 32, 34

Court Leet, 37

Curiosities of Popular Customs (Walsh), 39

Curse pole, 45

'Daisy', Mollie, called, 49

De Dea Syria, 39

Deal, 12, 14, 16, 17, 25, 37, 45, 49

Decay, cause of, 55

Dialect, Kent, 27, 55, 81, 82

Dictionary of The Kent Dialect (Parish & Shaw), 11, 35, 43, 47

Dictionary of Archaic and Provincial Words (Halliwell), 31

Dictionary of Obsolete and Provincial Words (Wright), 32

Disgavelled, 117, 118, 121, 122

Douce on the Morris dance, 84, 88, 89, 90

Dower, 116, 117, 119

Eastry, 49

Ekkehard, 37, 107

Elham, 54, 108

Elmsted, 54

English Dialect Dictionary, 43, 81

European Magazine, 13, 15, 17, 27 - 29, 35, 43 - 45, 50, 82, 94

Every Day Book (Hone), 22, 29, 31, 32, 36, 40, 78, 82

Evington, 51, 54

Fate, goddess of, 95, 96, 104

Faversham, 50, 55

Fays, 95, 96, 97, 98, 100, 104

Feien, die, *see* Fays

Finglesham, 49

Folk Lore Journal, 13, 75

Folklore, 86, 93, 102

Fools' dance, 90, 91

Frankalmoign, 115, 117, 118, 121, 122
Frey, 38
Friar Tuck, 84, 99
Gabriel's Hounds, 103
Gavelkind, 7, 12, 13, 112 - 124
Gentleman's Magazine, The, 27, 30, 31
Geschichte der deutschen Weihnacht (Tille), 105
Glamorganshire, 77, 78, 80
Gloucestershire, 79, 80
Godmersham, 27, 50, 55
Goodening, 42, 81, 82
Gore Street, Monkton, 16, 17, 21, 24
Gratuity placed in mouth of horse, 25, 54, 89
Guide to Coast of Kent (Walcott), 32
Hackelbernd (personification of Wild Huntsman), 96
Halle, 98, 100
Handbuch der deutschen Mythologie (Simrock), 103
Harbledown, 52
Hardres, Lower, 52, 53, 54, 89
Hardres, Upper, 53
Hastingleigh, 55
Haxey Hood, 85
Health Resort, 43, 45, 82
Herne, 38, 51, 52, 103
Highways and Byways in Kent (Jerrold), 47
Hildesheim, 92, 98
History of Kent (Dunkin), 30, 31, 81
History of Staffordshire (Plott), 75
Hoath, 24, 38, 49, 51, 112
Hobby horse, 13, 30 - 34, 39, 40, 42, 44, 75 - 77, 81, 84, 85, 87 - 89, 91, 93, 98, 106, 109
Hobelers, 31
Hob-Nob (Salisbury), 55, 76, 78, 87
Holla, Frau, 104
Hood, Robin, 16, 75, 84 - 93, 99, 104 - 106, 109
Hooded, 81
Hoodener, 23 - 25, 41 - 43, 52, 58, 60, 81, 85, 89
Hoodman, 43, 44
Hoppe (gothic), 81
Jockey, 15, 36, 46, 52, 110
Jule-buk, 102
Keble's Gazette, 46, 48, 50, 51, 76
Kent (Kilburne), 108
Kent Herald, 33
Kentish Express, 40, 41, 81, 82
Kentish Gazette, 33, 48
Kentish Men, 7, 112, 123
Kentish Note Book, The (Howell), 35, 36, 39
King Harold, 118
Kingscote (Glos.), 80
Klapperbock, 98, 100, 101, 102

Knight service, 114 - 122
Kuhn, Adalbert, 92, 94, 96, 97, 99, 103, 104, 105
Lancashire, 13, 44, 80
Latimer, Bishop, 86
Lays, &c., of Weald of Kent (Winser), 42
Lincolnshire, Marshland of, 79
Little John, 84, 86, 99
Lytell Geste, A, &c (Gutch), 84
Madingley Morris dancers, 89
Magic of the Horseshoe, The (Lawrence), 43
Maid Marian, 84, 85, 88, 91, 99, 109
Male heirs, 115, 117 - 119, 121
Margate, 16, 45, 46, 50, 51
Mari Llywd (Lywd), 13, 14, 15, 34, 77, 78, 108
Märkische Forschungen, 94, 96 - 98, 108
Märkische Sagen und Märchen, 94, 96, 98, 102, 104, 106
May games, 84, 85
Men of Kent, 7, 112, 123
Minehead Hobby Horse, 13, 73, 76, 77, 87
Minster (Thanet), 21, 33, 36, 48 - 50
'Moll' in Madingley Morris dancers, 89
Mollie, 16, 23 - 25, 49, 51, 52, 54, 57, 85, 88, 91, 102, 105, 110
Monkton, 16, 17, 21, 24, 35, 36, 48, 110
Morris dance, 12, 44, 66, 76, 84 - 91, 99, 105, 111, 112
Mumbles, The (Glam.), 78, 80
Musicians, 15, 24, 25, 45, 57, 89
Mystole, 53, 54
Myth Ritual and Religion, 39
Mythomistes, 90
Nackington, 53
Newton, (Glam.), 80
Niclas, knecht, 95, 104
Norddeutsche Sagen, &c. (Kuhn & Schwarz), 99
Northdown, 46, 47
Northwich (Cheshire), 42, 78
Notes & Queries, 32, 33, 34, 39, 44, 45, 82, 88, 105, 107, 108
Odin, 38, 39, 41, 44, 81, 82, 83, 94, 95
Odinin', 41, 82
Ogbourne St George (Wilts), 79
Old English Customs, &c. (Ditchfield), 42, 81
Old Hob, 78
Once a Week, 33
Ox, mimic, 102, 106
Padstow Hobby Horse, 74, 76, 77, 87, 98
Pen Ceffyl, 77
Penitential of Archbishop Theodore, 16, 38, 39, 105
Petham, 53, 55

Pivinton, Pluckley, 7, 94
Plough Bullocks, 79, 86
Plough Monday, 16, 79, 88
Pont Llew (Glam.), 77, 78
Popular Antiquities (Brand), 30, 32, 34, 43, 77, 84
Preston-next-Wingham, 51
Primitive Culture (Tylor), 103
Primogeniture, 118, 120, 121
Prophecies. &c. (Cobbe), 88
Puddledock, 54, 108
Raging Host, 95, 103
Ramsgate, 30, 32 - 34, 36, 40, 43 - 45, 50, 98
Reculver, 38, 51
Relics for the Curious, 28, 35, 36, 82
Restitution of Decayed Intelligence (Verstegan), 108
Revesby Morris dance, 75, 89
Rider on a White Horse, *see* Schimmelreiter
Rider, 16, 23, 24, 76, 94 - 101, 103, 104
Ruprecht, knecht, 92, 95, 98, 100, 102, 104
Sacking, 11, 14, 15, 23, 79, 85, 89, 107, 111
Saga Book of the Viking Club, The, 45, 47, 79
Sandwich, 45, 48, 83, 91
Sarre, 16, 24, 44, 48, 51, 57, 58, 110
Saxons (Kemble), 38
Schimmel, 94, 98 - 102, 104
Schimmelreiten, 101 - 102, 106
Schimmelreiter, 95, 97, 100 - 104
Scotland, Act of Parliament, 86
Shakespeare, Henry IV, 88
Sheep in tree, dead body of, 94
Sheep's skull, 80
Sheffield, 80
Slaughter customs, 102, 105, 106
Socage, 114 - 119
Song at Blean, hoodening, 52
Souling (Cheshire), 14, 15, 78, 102, 111
Sports and Pastimes, &c. (Strutt), 84, 85, 87, 89 - 91
St George, *see* Woden
St Nicholas-at-Wade, 12, 16, 17, 24, 35, 36, 48, 57, 58, 65, 110, 112
Staffan's ride, 102
Stelling, 54
Stourmouth, 51
Stourton (Wilts.), 79

Sturry, 51, 52
Swalecliffe, 52
Swarling, 55
T.P.'s Weekly, 47
Tenancy, 117, 119
Tenure, 114, 115, 117 - 119, 121, 122
Teutonic Mythology (Grimm), 95, 96
Thanet Advertiser, 33, 81
Thanet, 14, 16, 21 - 26, 28 - 30, 35 - 38, 40, 42, 44 - 51, 53, 55, 82, 89 - 91, 94, 112
Tilmanstone, 49
Tollett window, 84, 109
Updown, 48, 51
Upstreet, 51
Usedom, Isle of, 98, 100 - 102
Waggoner, 11, 15, 23, 24, 41, 110
Walmer, 12, 14, 16, 22, 24 - 26, 37, 38, 42, 49, 53, 54, 59, 60, 88, 89, 111, 112
Waltham, 53, 108
Wanesberge, see Woodnesborough,
Wassailing the orchards, 14, 107
Weald of Kent, 42, 55
Weaverham (Cheshire), 78
Weihnachten (Rietschel), 100, 102
Welsh Folk-Lore and Folk Stories (Trevelyan), 108
West Kent, 54, 111
Westbere, 93, 94
Whittlesey Strawbear, 102
Wild Huntsman, 96, 101, 103, 105
William the Conqueror, 7, 118
Wiltshire Archaeological Magazine, 79
Wiltshire Village, A, 79
Winsboro', *see* Woodnesborough
Woden horse (expression used), 28 - 31, 51, 81, 82, 99, 104, 109
Woden, 16, 17, 28, 29, 41, 44, 81 - 83, 91 - 100, 103 - 108
Woodnesborough, (variants of name), 108
Wooset (Wiltshire custom), 79
Word, near Sandwich, 48, 49
Wuotan Hruodperaht, 104
Yule and Christmas, &c. (Tille), 104 - 106
Zeitschrift für deutsches Alterthum (Haupt), 92, 97, 102, 104